The ABCs of Buddhism

If You Want to Be Happy, Focus on Giving

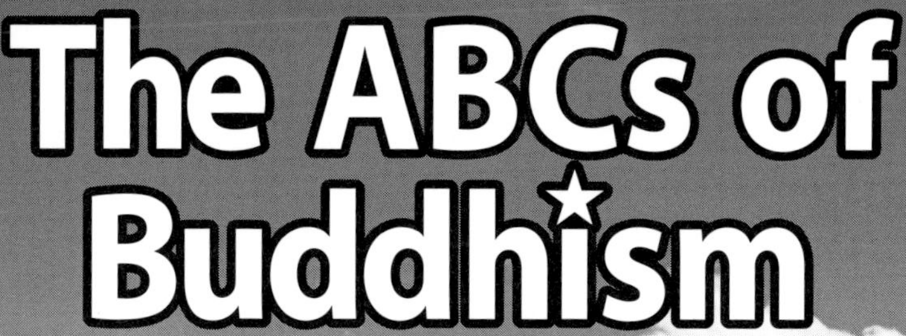

The ABCs of Buddhism

If You Want to Be Happy, Focus on Giving

By Hisashi Ota
Supervised by Kentaro Ito
Translated by Juliet Winters Carpenter

The ABCs of Buddhism: If You Want to Be Happy, Focus on Giving
By Hisashi Ota
Published by Ichimannendo Publishing, Inc. (IPI)
970 West 190th Street, Suite 920, Torrance, California 90502
info@i-ipi.com www.i-ipi.com

Supervised by Kentaro Ito
Translated by Juliet Winters Carpenter

Cover design by Kazumi Endo
Photograph by amanaimages

First edition, June 2016
Printed in Japan
20 19 18 17 16 1 2 3 4 5 6 7 8 9 10

This book was originally published in Japanese by Ichimannendo Publishing Co. Ltd. under the title of *Manga de wakaru bukkyo nyumon*.

Distributed in the United States and Canada by Atlas Books Distribution, a division of BookMasters, Inc.
30 Amberwood Parkway, Ashland, Ohio 44805
1-800-Booklog www.atlasbooks.com

Distributed in Japan by Ichimannendo Publishing Co. Ltd.
2-4-5F Kanda-Ogawamachi, Chiyoda-ku, Tokyo 101-0052
info@10000nen.com www.10000nen.com

Library of Congress Control Number: 2015960635
ISBN 978-0-9898477-2-8

ISBN 978-4-925253-98-7

Contents

Introducing the cast

Your merry classmates

Mr. Suzuki

He can teach you all kinds of things about Buddhism in great detail.

Ichiro

A lively, carefree kid with a hearty appetite, and the class clown.

Hikari

A diligent pupil, she is a cheerful, perky girl.

Naoki

An easygoing guy.

Masako

She loves fashion.

Tatsuki

A beacon of intelligence?

Lesson 1
Precious Life

Why a single human life outweighs the earth

Life is something you need to think about for yourself!

Aw, c'mon. Help a guy out.

Why do we have to write about such a hard topic anyhow?!

Must be because lately so many people show no respect for life.

Some people kill others or take their own lives over the littlest things ...

That is so sad!
Hmm ...

But after we die we get another chance, right? Like a RESET BUTTON on a game?

3

So when you die, you get reborn and start a new life! Right?
?

That can't be right.
Uh, don't think so.

Buddhism even has a word for it—"reincarnation."

It's not that easy. You don't get reborn human right away after you die.

Hang on, Ichiro!
Born again as a human?

That's why Buddhism teaches, "To be born human is extremely rare and precious, so you must be glad!"
Huh? You don't?
Huh ...

Say! Do you kids know the parable of the blind turtle and the log? It's in the *Miscellaneous Agama Sutra*.
No! Tell us.
One day Buddha asked his disciple Annan a question.

What do you think about having been born human?

I feel extremely fortunate.

How fortunate, exactly?

Um, well ...

Then Buddha told the following story.

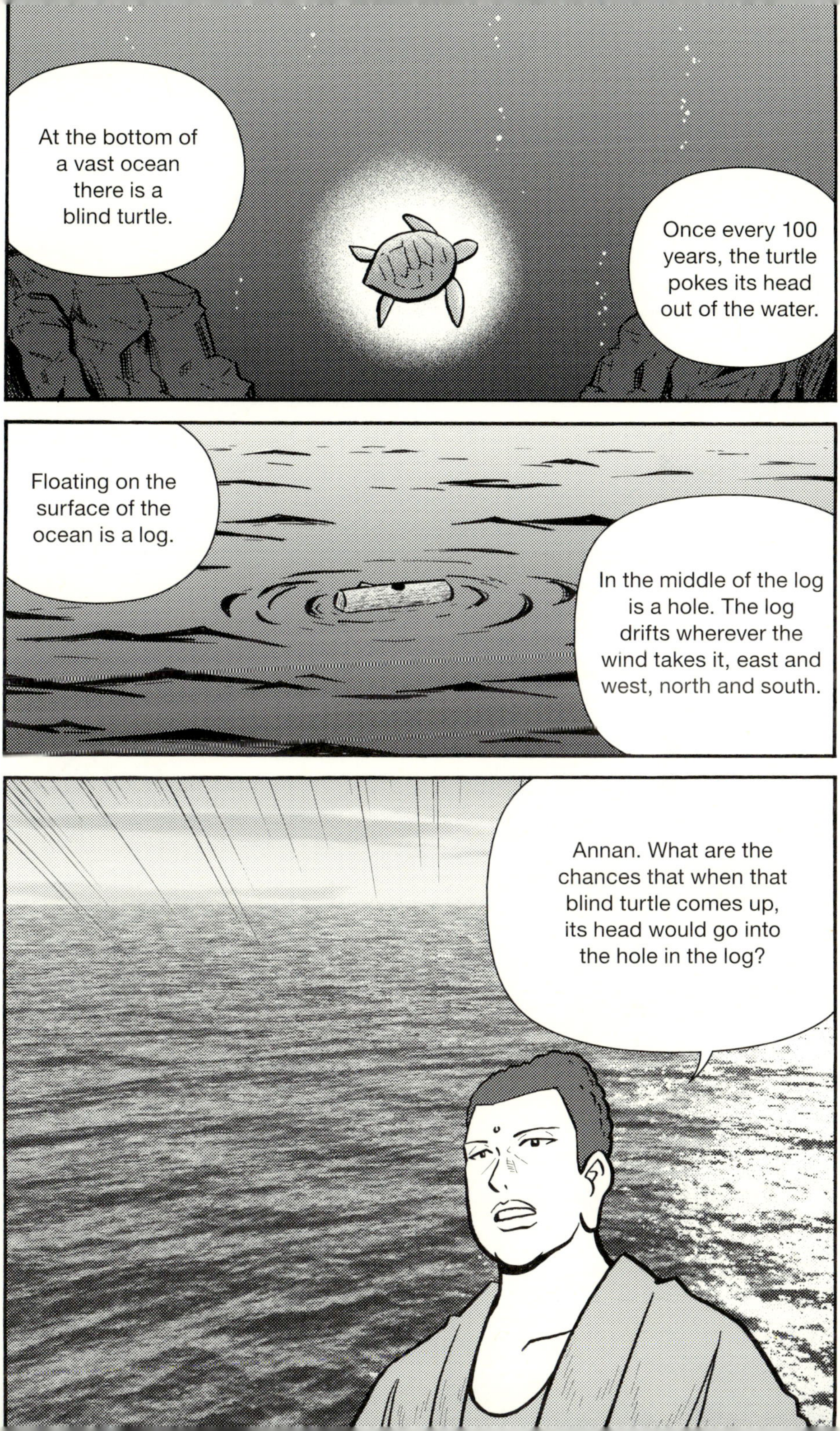

Annan. What are the chances that when that blind turtle comes up, its head would go into the hole in the log?

...... !

Would you say it was impossible?

Master, such a thing could hardly happen!

W-well, no ...

Perhaps once in a million billion trillion years such a thing might happen, but it would be so rare it would be practically impossible!

True.

But Annan, for us to be born human is even more difficult than for that turtle to poke its head through the hole in the log!
Human life is rare and precious.

That's what Buddha taught.

Yikes!
That's mind-blowing!

Is it THAT hard to be born human??
?

Think about it. How many millions of different kinds of life forms live on this earth?

How many fish swim in all the oceans and rivers?

They say one sunfish lays 300 MILLION eggs at a time.

Add in all the ants, flies, and other insects, and the number is astronomical!

You could have been born one of them.

Hrm.
Being born human is really something to be thankful for!

That's why people in rescue squads and trauma wards give up their holidays.

Yeah! Like on TV, in the show *ER*!

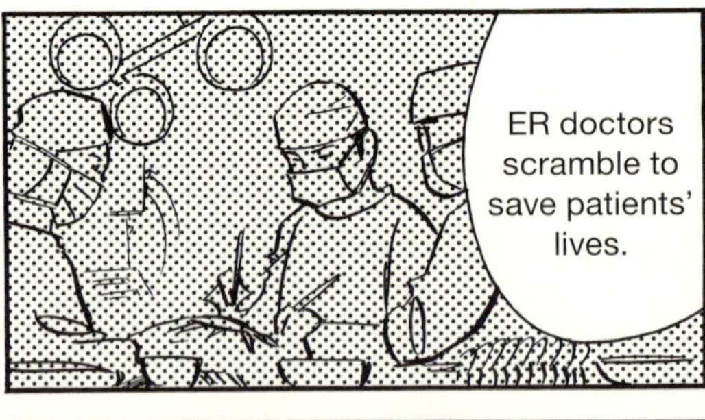
ER doctors scramble to save patients' lives.

I wanna be a doctor someday!
You? Better start doing your homework once in a while!

Yet even though life is so precious, lots of people easily commit murder or suicide.

Yes, it's extremely sad.

Just hearing about the preciousness of human life doesn't make them happy.

To them, life is so hard they wish they'd never been born!

Huh.
So just knowing how hard it is to be born human isn't enough to make people truly glad ...

Right. That's it.

Listen carefully. Life isn't always fun.

It's full of stress and pain.
Yeah, like this homework ...

But Buddha taught us why we need to go on living despite such difficulties. He taught what everyone wants to know, the meaning of life.
Huh? He did?

Buddha taught that being born human and listening to Buddhism are extremely difficult.
Human form is difficult to obtain;
Now I have already obtained it.
Buddhism is difficult to hear;
Now I have already heard it.

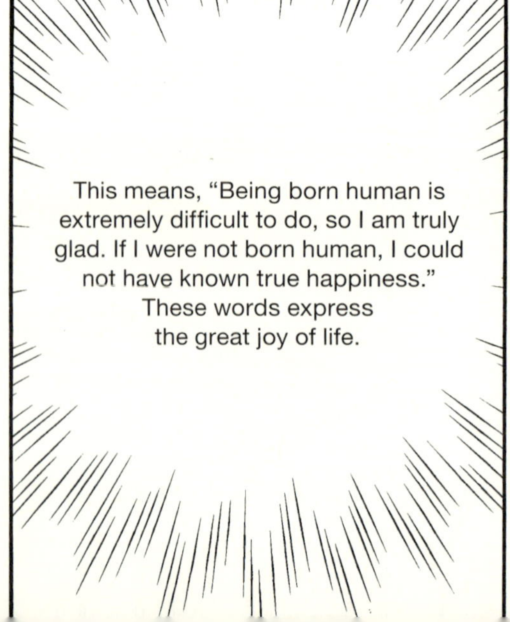
This means, "Being born human is extremely difficult to do, so I am truly glad. If I were not born human, I could not have known true happiness." These words express the great joy of life.

Attaining that joy is the purpose of life.

The purpose of life ...

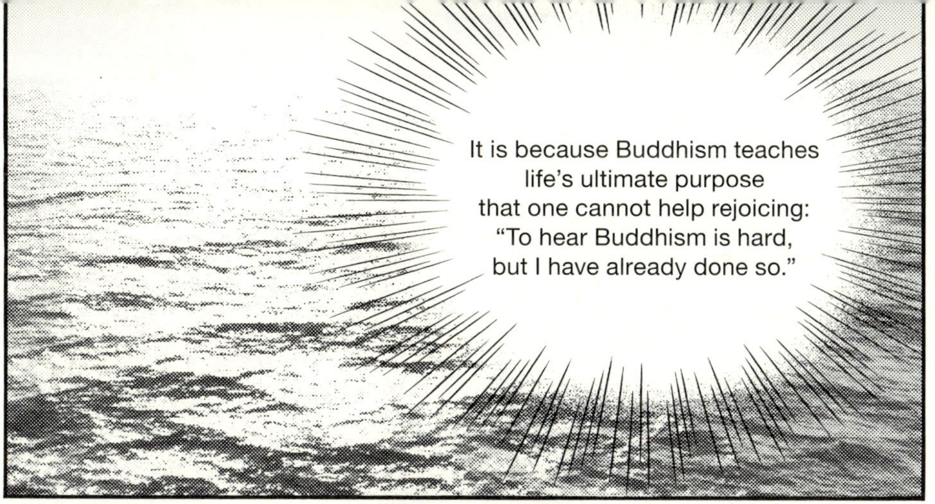
It is because Buddhism teaches
life's ultimate purpose
that one cannot help rejoicing:
"To hear Buddhism is hard,
but I have already done so."

Oh, I get it!

And everyone's life
has the same purpose,
so everyone's life
is equally precious!

People's lives
really ARE precious!

That's why they say
a single life
outweighs the earth.

It's cool
to be glad
you were born!

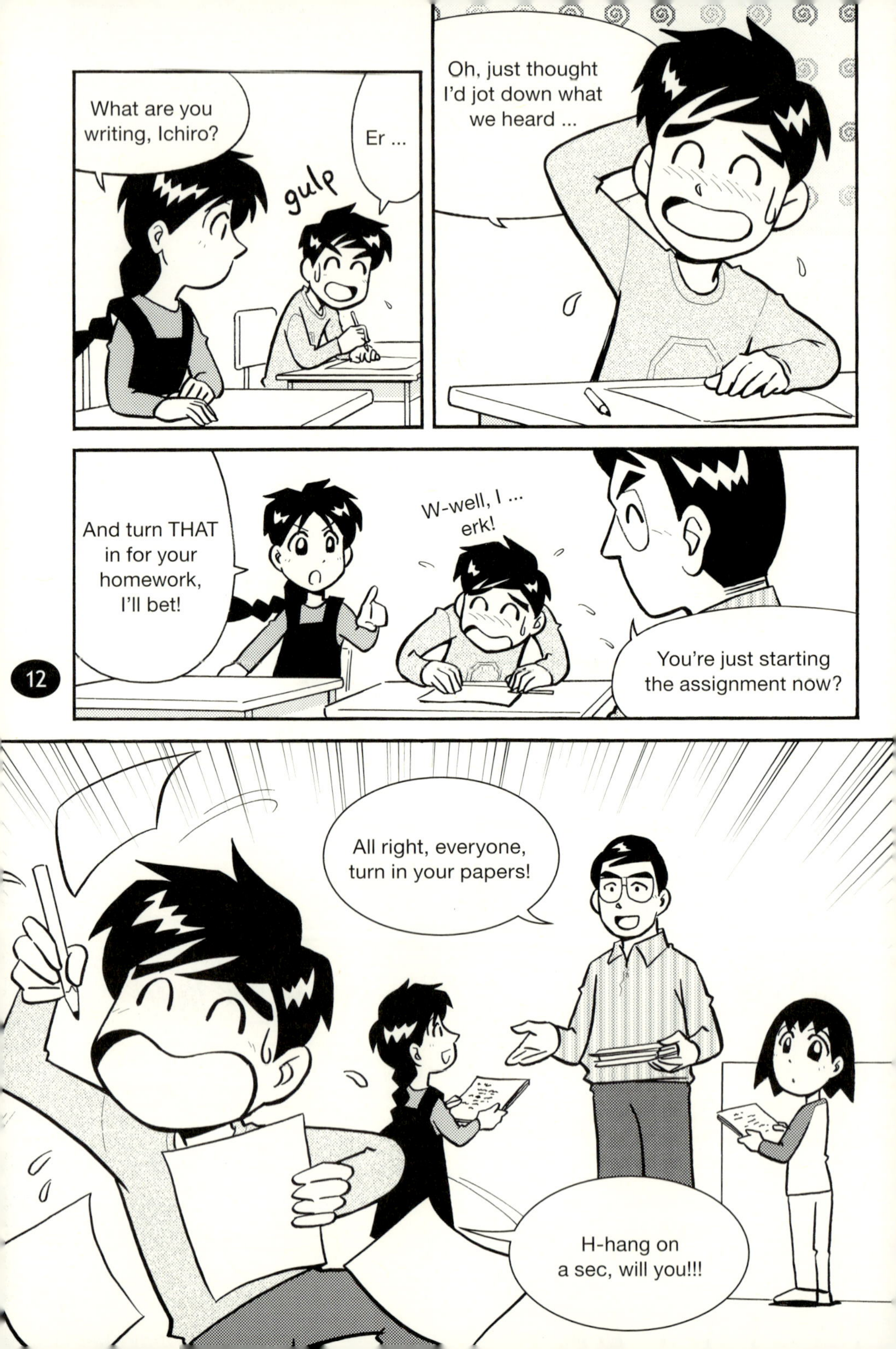

What are you writing, Ichiro?
gulp
Er ...

All right, everyone, turn in your papers!
H-hang on a sec, will you!!!

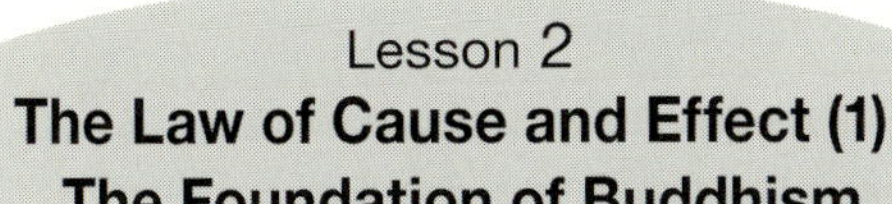

Lesson 2

The Law of Cause and Effect (1): The Foundation of Buddhism

The principle that makes a happy future

How DARE You!!

Scary!

Calm down, calm down ...

FWUMP

Ahem.
The foundation of Buddhism is the "law of cause and effect."
Hey, it's the teacher! Mr. Suzuki!

Where did you come from?

I took shelter here from the rain before you did!

So tell us—what's the "law of cause and effect"?
OK!

First, a "law" is a truth that never changes in all the three temporal worlds and ten directions.
Come again?

15

The "three worlds" are the past, the present, and the future.
In other words, "anytime."
The "ten directions" are north, south, east, west; the directions in between; and up and down.
In short, "anywhere."
THE THREE WORLDS
THE TEN DIRECTIONS

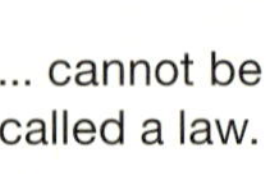

CAUSE

EFFECT

A "cause" is a reason for something, and an "effect" is a result.

Really? I bet some things happen for no reason.

Mm ... like what?
Well, suppose there's a plane crash.

We're over the crash site. The plane has sunk into the ocean, and the cockpit voice recorder cannot be retrieved.

The cause of the accident is unknown.
See? They can't find any cause.

WHIR
WHIR

But just because they can't find the cause doesn't mean there isn't one.

Never in a million trillion times could there be an effect without a cause.
SOMETHING caused the crash.
Oh, right ...

Here is what Buddha taught regarding the relationship between the cause and effect of our fate, our greatest concern.

Here "cause" means our actions, and "effect" means our destiny or fate.
Good cause, good effect.
Bad cause, bad effect.
Own cause, own effect.

Who is your DESTINY?
The perfect partner
Horoscope
What is your FATE?
Today's FORTUNE
Know your DESTINY!!
"Destiny," "fortune,"— those words come up a lot in magazines ...

So you're going to tell us what decides our destiny?!
That I'd like to know!

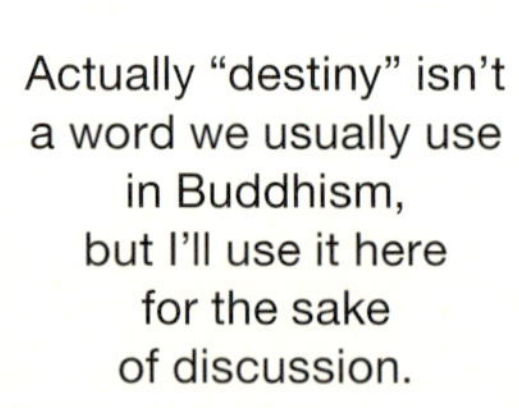

Actually "destiny" isn't a word we usually use in Buddhism, but I'll use it here for the sake of discussion.

Right. What we each want to know most is our destiny!

We want good results, not bad ones. How do we make that happen?

Buddha revealed the answer by teaching this law.

What decides a person's fortune?

If we do good deeds, we get good results.

And if we do bad deeds, we get bad results.

Yes.
It's like farming ...
Sow radish seeds,
and you'll get radishes.
Sow watermelon seeds, you'll get watermelons.

TAKE2
But don't good causes ever lead to bad results, or the other way around?

Impossible.

I planted watermelon seeds but I got radishes!

I planted pumpkin seeds but I got cucumbers!

What could be stranger than that? If we didn't know what would come up, we'd never know what seed to sow.

Wonder what'll sprout this time ...
Farming doesn't work that way.

No sir. Buddhism tells us that the law of cause and effect is a universal truth, no exceptions.

Wow!
I want good results—
I sure don't want
any bad ones.
This stuff
is important!
My,
aren't we
serious!

Gimme a break.
It IS serious!
My fate depends
on it!

What's
with
that look
in your
eyes??
Mm ...

I didn't
say that!
Ooh, you think
my eyes
are pretty?

21

Yes!
That's
the law
of cause
and effect.
Got it?

Okay, you two!
As you see,
no one
can be happy
unless they do
good deeds,
and doing
bad deeds
invites misfortune!

drip
drip

22

Will wonders never cease?!

Lay off, will you! Just because I got motivated ...

OK. Off to Ichiro's house!

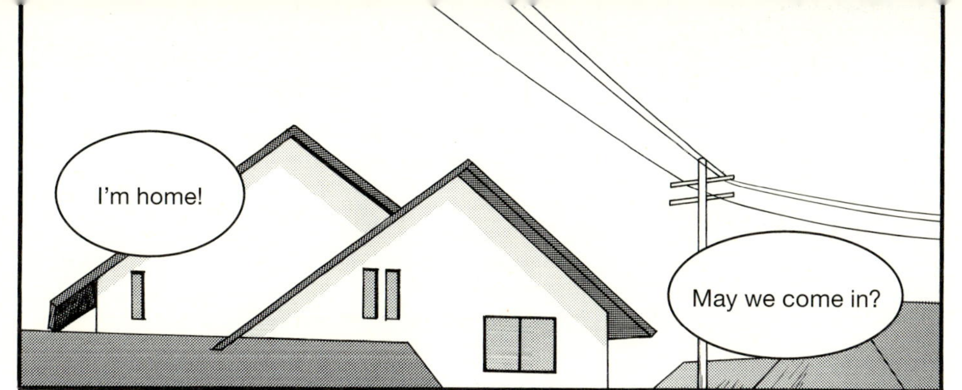

Lesson 3

The Law of Cause and Effect (2): Own Causes, Own Effects

Don't hate people or hold grudges.

Mom, I brought everyone here to study.

Love ♥ Sonata

Mom?

What's this?

crunch

She's wrapped up in a soap opera.

LARDY CRACKERS

You expect me to eat this crap?

CRASH

Aaagh!

Bring me some booze. NOW!
OK ...

Dear, you shouldn't drink so much ...
GLUG
GLUG

Urrg
Shut up! I lost money on the ponies. Fork over some more.

We don't have that kind of money.
Then go out and get some!

Oh, you're so mean ...
Oh no ...

Hey, Mom! Listen!
That poor woman! She's so hardworking, kindhearted, and devoted ...

GRRR!
But that husband of hers!

He hardly does a lick of work, just gambles away his wife's hard-earned money ...
CHOMP CHOMP
LARDY CRACKERS
Hey Mom! Come on!

Her suffering is all his fault!
ROOOAR!

He's to blame!
Mom, get a grip!
RATTLE RATTLE
Ack ...

The teacher's here, too.
What? Oh, how embarrassing!

25

Why didn't you say something?!
SLAP
I tried, I tried!

THE LAW OF CAUSE AND EFFECT
Well, ma'am, I understand how you feel.
Let's review. Who can explain the law of cause and effect?

CAUSE = ACTION

EFFECT = FATE

Um, "cause" means our actions, and "effect" means our fate.

It means everyone's fate is the result of the deeds they do.

Say I have too much alcohol and get drunk ...
Bartender, fill 'er up!
Hic
Phut
Whiskey

The person next to me isn't affected.
Funny. I drink and drink, but I don't get drunk!
GLUG GLUG
What's goin' on? Somebody, help!
URGH ...
It'd be scary if that ever happened for real!

If you study hard, YOUR grades go up, not your friend's.
Better grades, here I come!
ZZZ
PASS!

Woohoo!! You studied hard, so my grades went up!
100
BOING
?
Why?
This is crazy!
20

That would be "other cause, own effect."

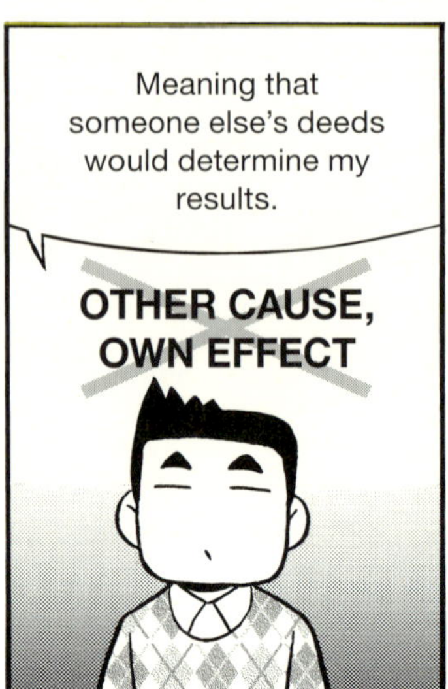
Meaning that someone else's deeds would determine my results.
OTHER CAUSE, OWN EFFECT

Right, Naoki. But that never happens. "Own cause, own effect" always holds true.

That's obvious.
Huh!
Hmm. You think so??

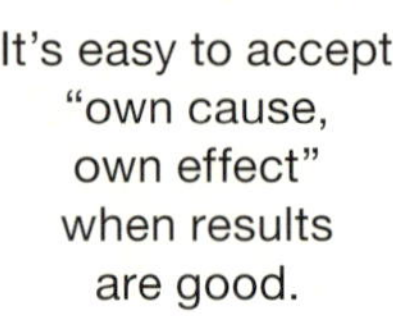
It's easy to accept "own cause, own effect" when results are good.

It's very hard to accept it when bad things happen to us.

YOU make my life miserable!
She puts me through hell!

We tend to blame others and hate them.

Yeah, I guess once in a while ...
You always do!

It's like the old saying: "The thief blames the rope that binds him."
What's that mean?

In the old days thieves were bound with rope.
Rats!
Today police use handcuffs.

Bound fast, the thief can't move freely ...
This rope is the cause of my suffering. Without it, I'd be free!
... and blames the rope.

What do you think about that?
He's a fool.

I mean, what got him tied up was his own actions. He should blame himself.

BINNG!
I get it! Blaming others—like "It's all his fault!" or "She's to blame!"—makes us just like the thief blaming the rope!

That's right, Hikari. All the rope in the world wouldn't bother him if he didn't steal.

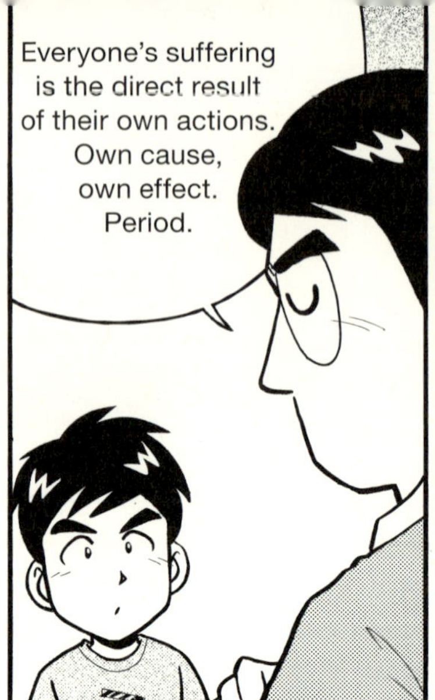
Everyone's suffering is the direct result of their own actions. Own cause, own effect. Period.

H-hold on! What about the wife in that TV show?

Now that you mention it ...
Who, me?
Isn't she suffering because of her husband?

It's natural to think so, but the cause of her suffering is within her.
Why?

No matter how awful he is, if she hadn't married him, she wouldn't have suffered so much.

There are plenty of men in the world.
Of all people, she chose HIM to fall in love with.

If she'd married someone like you, things would've been different!
Save the flattery!

30

Anyway, without a doubt the cause lies in her own past deeds.

Well, what about her husband?! Don't tell me he's got nothing to do with it!
Calm down, Mom.

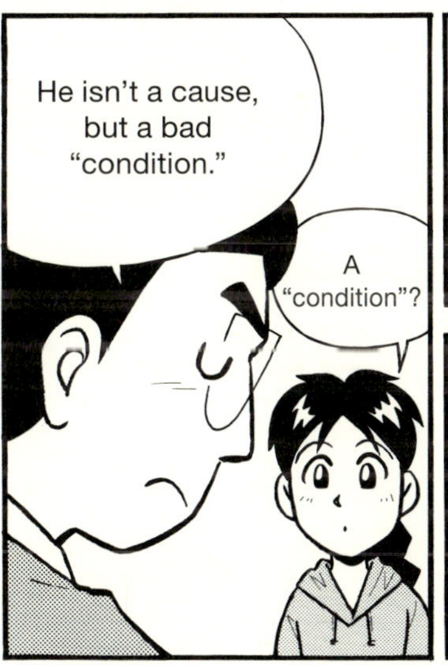
He isn't a cause, but a bad "condition."
A "condition"?

Unless a cause and conditions come together, an effect does not arise.
CONDITION
CAUSE

31

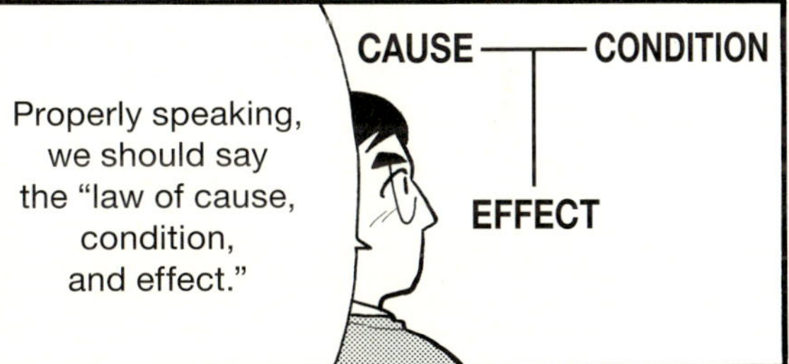
Properly speaking, we should say the "law of cause, condition, and effect."
CAUSE
CONDITION
EFFECT

For example, the cause of rice is rice seeds.

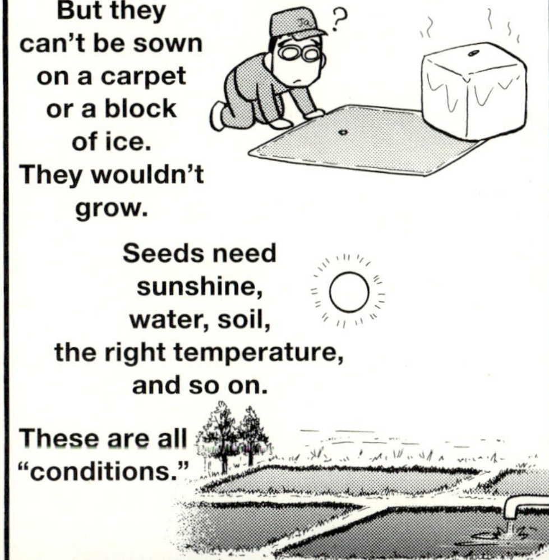
But they can't be sown on a carpet or a block of ice. They wouldn't grow.
Seeds need sunshine, water, soil, the right temperature, and so on.
These are all "conditions."

Only when a cause and conditions come together will rice grow as a result.

Makes sense.

So the cause was within the wife herself, and the husband was a bad condition.

You should be! Shame on you for being such a disgraceful condition!

Urgh ... I'm sorry, I'm sorry!

Mom! Calm down, please!!!

RATTLE

RATTLE

There's more to come about the law of cause and effect!

Lesson 4

The Law of Cause and Effect (3): Karmic Power

Gosh, the cherry blossoms are gorgeous!

My own actions determine my future.

This is Mt. Yoshino in Nara, Japan.

yum
yum
Good grief! Dumplings mean more to you than blossoms.

Never mind. Let's review what we know about the law of cause and effect.

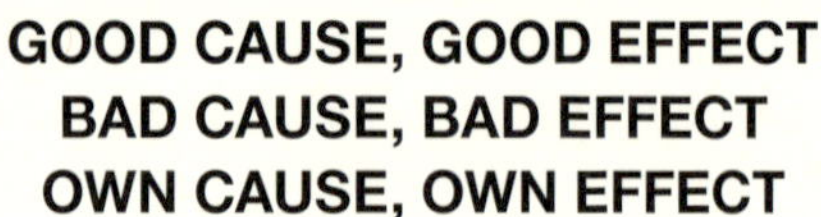
GOOD CAUSE, GOOD EFFECT
BAD CAUSE, BAD EFFECT
OWN CAUSE, OWN EFFECT

I know! "Good causes produce good effects. Bad causes produce bad effects. Own causes produce own effects."

34

And "causes" means our actions, what we do.

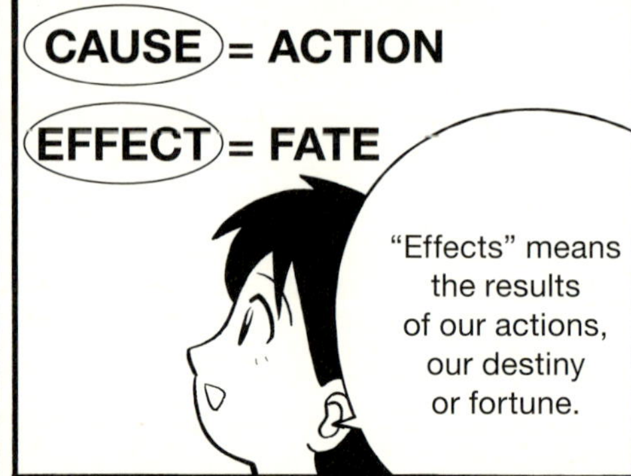
CAUSE = ACTION
EFFECT = FATE
"Effects" means the results of our actions, our destiny or fortune.

Yes. So good deeds bring good fortune, and bad deeds, bad fortune.
And my own actions determine my fate.
Mm ...

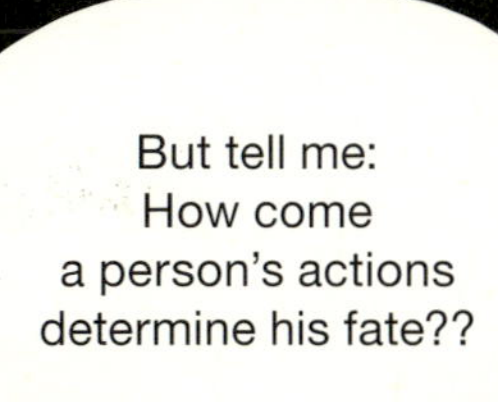
But tell me:
How come
a person's actions
determine his fate??

KARMA
OK, listen.
In Buddhism,
another word
for deeds
is "karma."

INDESTRUCTIBLE KARMIC POWER
Karma remains as
an invisible power
that never fades.
It's indestructible.

Power,
you said?
ripple
Power
to create our fate,
he means.

35

Yes.
And that power
is kept
in our "store
consciousness."
Our ...
what?

Our "store
consciousness,"
which is our
eternal life.
STORE CONSCIOUSNESS
It comes from
Indian words
meaning
"storehouse"
and "mind."

So it's like a storehouse within you that holds all your karmic power limitlessly.

You just don't see storehouses anymore, do you ...
Like this!
Stop talking like an old fart!

How can it keep storing without limit?
Think of a computer. You input data.

But you're not inserting objects into the computer.
You're inputting invisible energy.

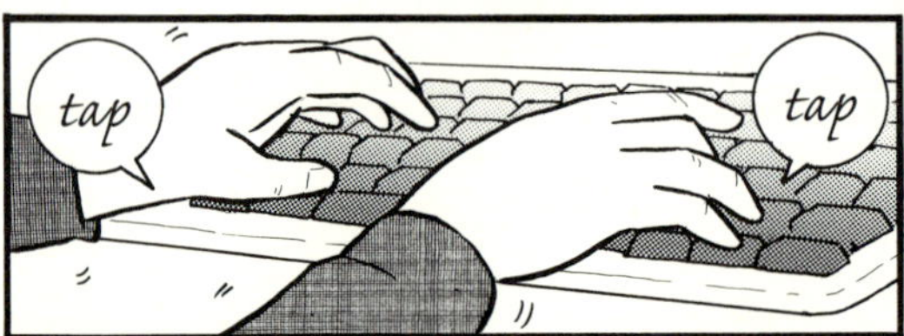
tap
tap

That's why so much data fits on such a small disk.

Our small brains hold a lot of data too!
That they do!
Ooh!

A scholar's brain can retain the contents of an entire library.
Holy smokes.

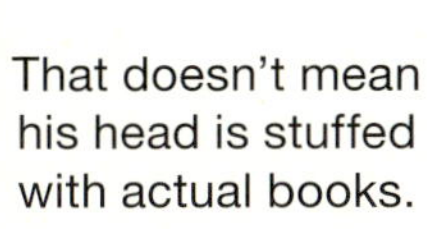
That doesn't mean his head is stuffed with actual books.

The contents are stored invisibly.
Right.

That reminds me of a poem!
Year after year
cherry blossoms bloom again
on Mt. Yoshino.
Split the tree and look inside—
where are all the flowers?

Every spring, cherry blossoms come out on Mt. Yoshino.

But go there in winter, and there's nothing but withered-looking trees.

*Japanese Criminal Law Article 261 states that chopping another person's cherry tree constitutes property damage.

So conditions aren't enough. Without a cause, there's no result.

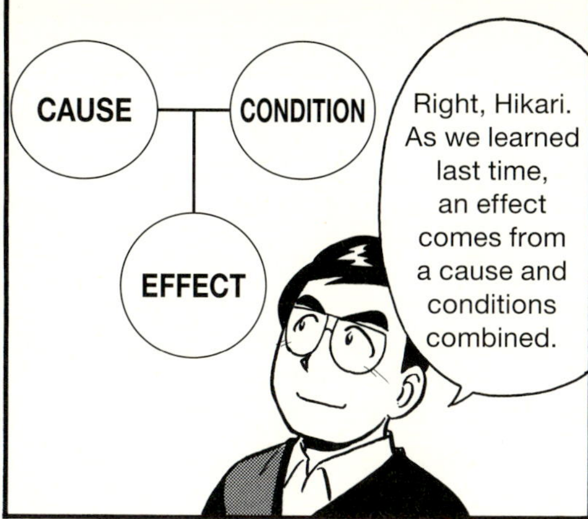
CAUSE
CONDITION
EFFECT
Right, Hikari. As we learned last time, an effect comes from a cause and conditions combined.

When there's a long winter and spring is late in coming, the blossoms are late too.
Whoooosh
Apr.
In that case there is a cause, but one condition is delayed.

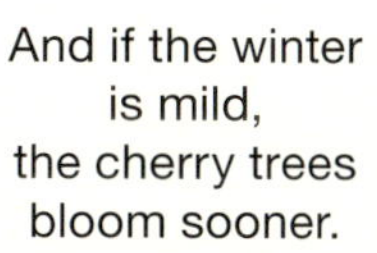
And if the winter is mild, the cherry trees bloom sooner.

That's because the condition came early.

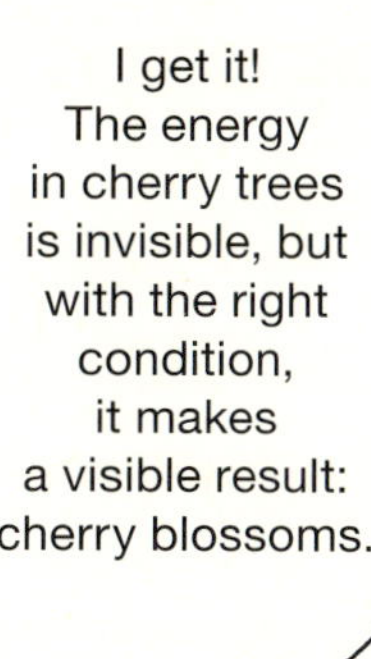
I get it! The energy in cherry trees is invisible, but with the right condition, it makes a visible result: cherry blossoms.

Karmic power is invisible too, but it combines with conditions to produce our fate.

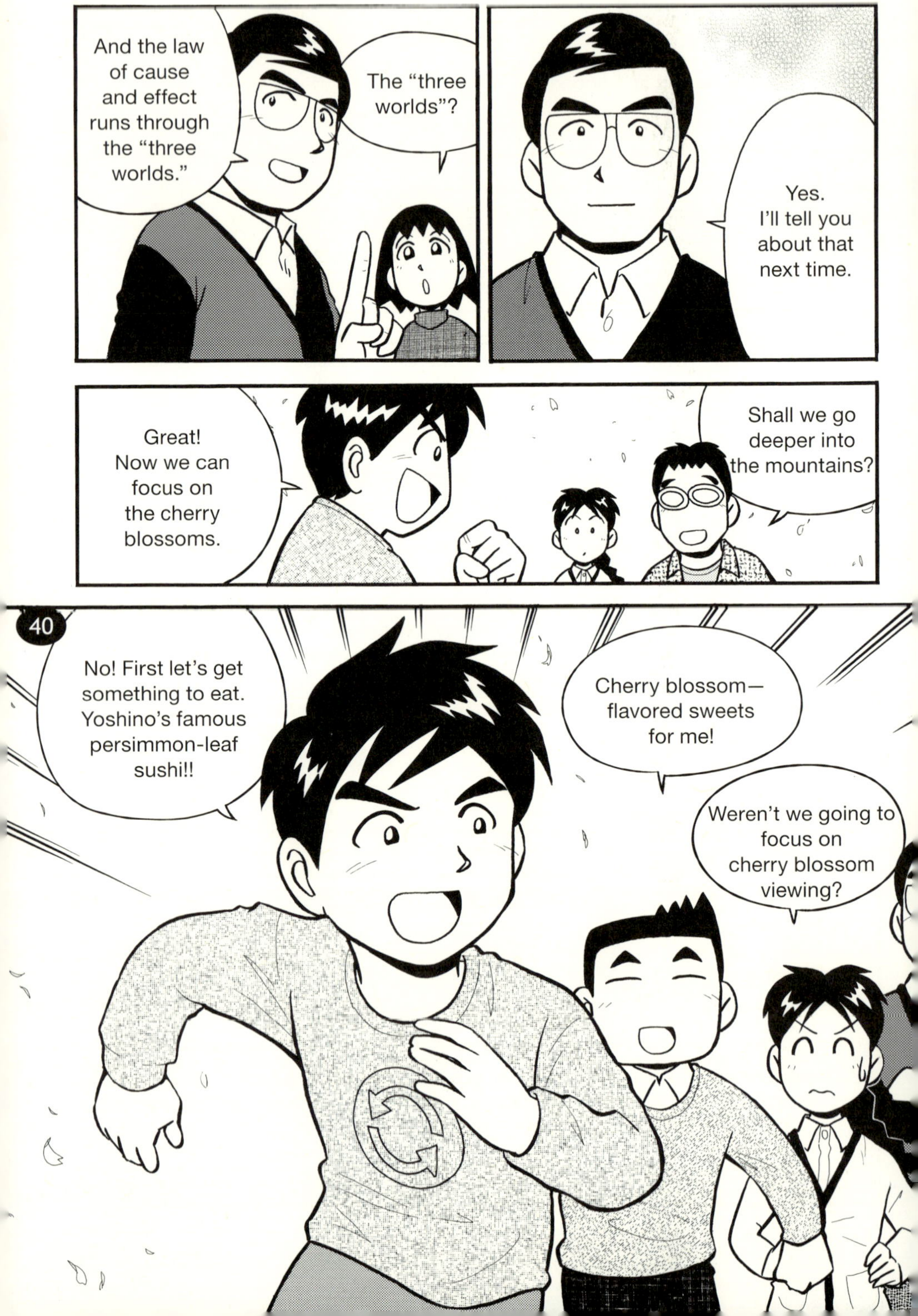

No! First let's get something to eat. Yoshino's famous persimmon-leaf sushi!!

Cherry blossom–flavored sweets for me!

Weren't we going to focus on cherry blossom viewing?

Lesson 5

The Law of Cause and Effect (4): Cause and Effect in the Three Worlds

The present is the key to the past and the future.

41

Ah, the law
of cause
and effect.

GOOD CAUSE, GOOD EFFECT
BAD CAUSE, BAD EFFECT
OWN CAUSE, OWN EFFECT

"Cause" refers
to our deeds
or actions.

"Effect" is
our fate.

And my own
actions
determine
my fate.

Mm.
A sharp insight,
Ichiro.
Mr.
Suzuki!

THE THREE WORLDS
The law
of cause
and effect
runs through the
three worlds.

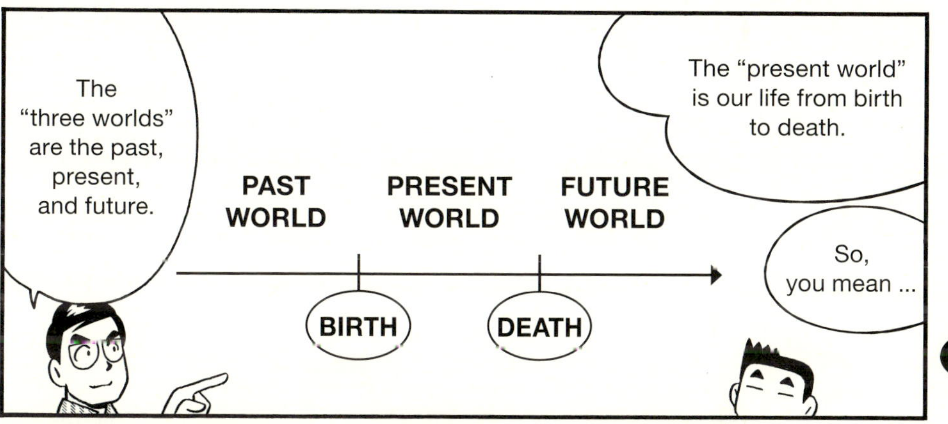
The
"three worlds"
are the past,
present,
and future.
PAST WORLD
PRESENT WORLD
FUTURE WORLD
BIRTH
DEATH
The "present world"
is our life from birth
to death.
So,
you mean ...

Why is anyone
born a boy
or a girl?

Why was I
born in Japan
and not Korea
or China?

No matter how much
you think about it,
our fate is
incomprehensible.

Even if you're born in Japan, which city makes a huge difference!
Not the same!

If the timing of my birth was different, I might have gone to war.

I was born in the third year of Taisho (1914).
And think of all the different periods in history, too ...

All such results are determined by our deeds in our past lives.
Children born to the same parents have different faces, personalities, and talents.
The past creates the present.

Take someone's life and you get the death penalty.

Yes, and the present creates the future.
PRESENT WORLD
FUTURE WORLD
DEATH
CAUSE
EFFECT

But even if someone took 10 lives, or 100, he can be put to death only once.
I hereby sentence you to die 10 times.
bang bang
Get real.

So then, when will he face the consequences for the other nine or 99 murders he committed?

Hmm. Think so?
Once he's dead, case closed.

How about this? Say a job pays $100 for a day's work.
I'll work hard!

I worked 10 days.
You only get $100.

You worked 100 days, but it's still just $100.
Here.
That's crazy! For 10 days' work I should get $1000, and for 100 days, $10,000!!!

So you see, if causes are different, the results should also be different.

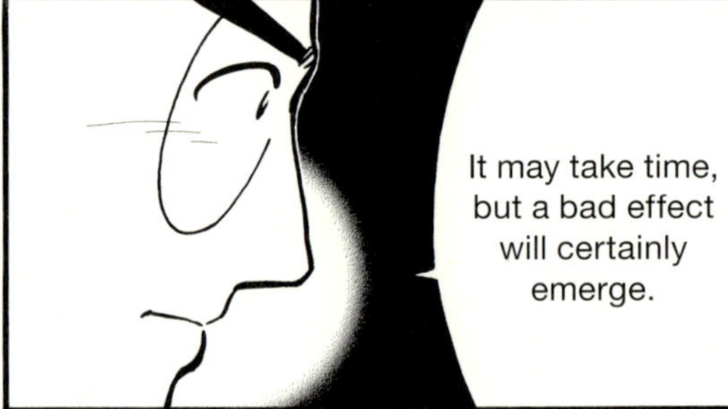

If you want to know past causes, look at present effects.

If you want to know future effects, look at present causes.

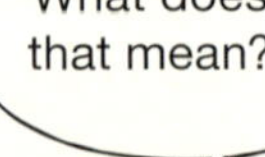

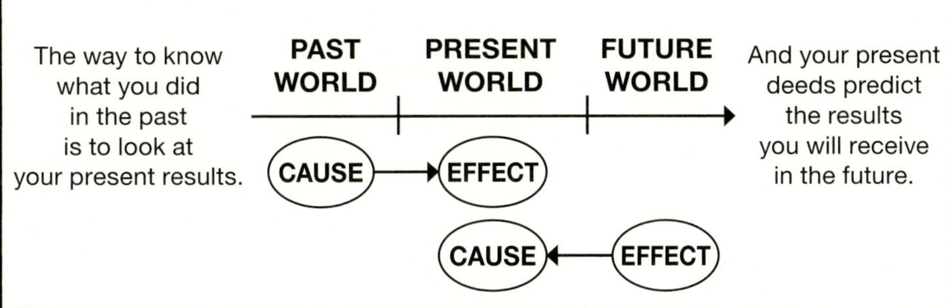
The way to know what you did in the past is to look at your present results.
PAST WORLD
PRESENT WORLD
FUTURE WORLD
CAUSE
EFFECT
CAUSE
EFFECT
And your present deeds predict the results you will receive in the future.

Someone with good grades now is someone who studied hard in the past!
No need to rub it in.

Someone who's lazy now and makes no effort can't expect good results in the future.

So looking deeply into the present reveals both the past and the future.
The key that unlocks the past and the future is the present.

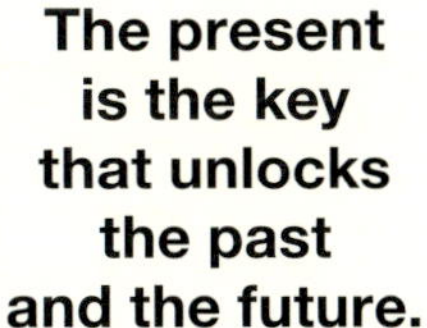
The present is the key that unlocks the past and the future.

Elementary.

That's why Buddhism teaches us so much about the present self.
Right.

RUBBISH

"Discard" means to get rid of something, "practice" to do something.

Doing bad things brings bad results on your head. Whatever you do, you are the one who harvests the results.

GOOD CAUSE, GOOD EFFECT

BAD CAUSE, BAD EFFECT

OWN CAUSE, OWN EFFECT

This ends the lesson on the law of cause and effect.
OK! Let's all try our best from now on!
You're rarin' to go, huh?
Anyway, first things first. Let's eat!
~growl
Let's have a Korean food party!!
I want some Korean dumplings.
Korean barbecued chicken for me.
All you people think about is eating!!!
Whew ... this kimchi is really spicy!!
Here you go! Dig in!
eek!!

Lesson 6

Six Good Deeds (1):
The Importance of Doing Good

What is a good deed?

Hey, how about getting off the floor and doing some homework with me?

Fluhhh
Thanks, I'll pass ...

If you don't do your homework, you'll get in trouble!

I knowww ... but I caaan't ...
Sigh
When ARE you going to do it?

flop
Like they say ... "All things come to he who waits."
flop

If I just wait, something good will happen!!
yum
Oh, for goodness' sake ...

If you want good results, get up and plant some good seeds!
Snap out of it!
SLIIIDE
Haaah ...

One day Bai Juyi, famous as a poet and a scholar of Confucianism, passed under the tree.

Let's have a bit of fun!

Hey, up there!
Isn't it dangerous
to sit
in a tall tree
with your
eyes closed??

It is you
who is in danger!

Hmm?!

Seems this is
an exceptional
monk ...
I am the
insignificant
Bai Juyi.
Might I ask
your name,
good monk?

I am the
insignificant
monk
Bird's Nest.

Ah, so I am
addressing
the famous
Master
Bird's Nest?

I am happy
to meet you!
Tell me one thing,
if you will:
In a nutshell,
what is it that
Buddhism
teaches?

Refrain from all forms of evil, and pursue good. This is Buddhism.
In other words, "Quit doing bad deeds, and do good deeds."

Hah!

Hee-hee!
Even a three-year-old child knows that!

Bird's Nest shot back ...
An infant of three knows it, but even an old man of eighty finds it hard to carry out!

Even little kids know they should do good, but grown-ups still can't really do that, right?
Hmm ...

You know, the foundation of Buddhism is the law of cause and effect.

Good causes yield good results, bad causes yield bad results, own causes yield own results. This holds true anytime and anywhere.

Do good deeds, and good things will happen!
Do bad deeds, and you're headed for misfortune.

Like we learned before.
You are sure to reap the results of the seeds you sow.

If you really understood, you would!
....
Yeah, but ... yeah, but ...

If you understood the law of cause and effect full well, you'd naturally quit doing bad deeds and start doing good deeds!

Are you being difficult on purpose?
Easy to say "good deeds," but ... just what should we do?
Hrmph

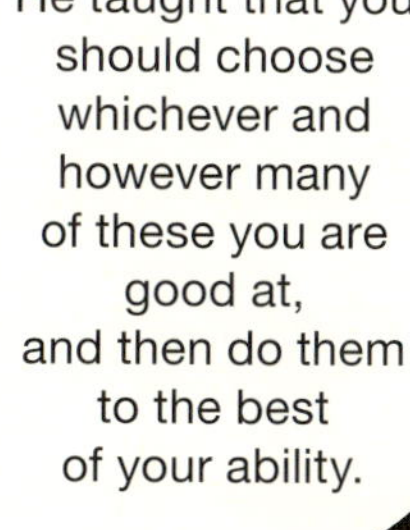

THE SIX PARAMITAS

GIVING
(KINDNESS)

DISCIPLINE
(KEEPING PROMISES)

FORBEARANCE
(PATIENCE)

DILIGENCE
(EFFORT)

CONTEMPLATION
(SELF-REFLECTION)

WISDOM
(SELF-CULTIVATION)

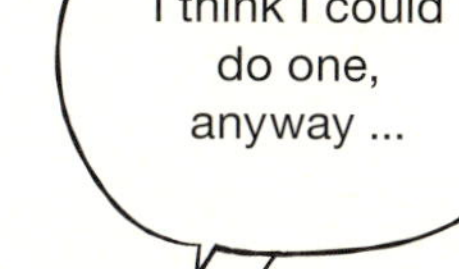

Well,
let's go
through them
one by one.
First,
"giving ..."
Mr.
Suzuki!
We've run
out of pages
for this issue.
Who's
this
guy?
Oh dear.
Well,
it'll have to
wait till
next time.
Yay!
Then we're done
for today ...
flop
flop
There he
goes again,
the lazybones!
Let's leave
Ichiro here
and go over
to my house
to work on
our homework!
Woohoo!
Hikari's house
is nice and
comfy!
And
there's
ice cream
too!
What?!
Wait for me!!
SWISH
Getting you
motivated
was simple

Lesson 7

Six Good Deeds (2): Giving 1

A poor person's one light outshines a millionaire's 10,000.

59

THE SIX PARAMITAS

GIVING (KINDNESS)
DISCIPLINE (KEEPING PROMISES)
FORBEARANCE (PATIENCE)
DILIGENCE (EFFORT)
CONTEMPLATION (SELF-REFLECTION)
WISDOM (SELF-CULTIVATION)

But—what if you haven't got resources or money to give to people?

But you know, the value of giving doesn't depend on the amount.

One day she went to listen to Buddha deliver a sermon.
The hall was brightly lit with oil lamps that people from all over town had brought as offerings.

How I wish I could offer a lamp, too!

Oh ...

Her intentions were pure, but oil was expensive, and she couldn't afford to buy any.

One day Nanda received a bit of money from a compassionate person. She went straight to an oil seller.
pitapat

You want to buy enough oil for one lamp?!

Please give me something!

Don't waste my time. This isn't nearly enough.

STARE
You're poor, I can tell by looking. Surely you've got better ways to use the money.

Why would you want oil that much??
SWISH
Please, I beg of you!

What?! To offer to Sakyamuni Buddha?

Actually ...

Well, well.
In that case
I'll give you
a special
discount.

Oh,
th-thank you
so much!

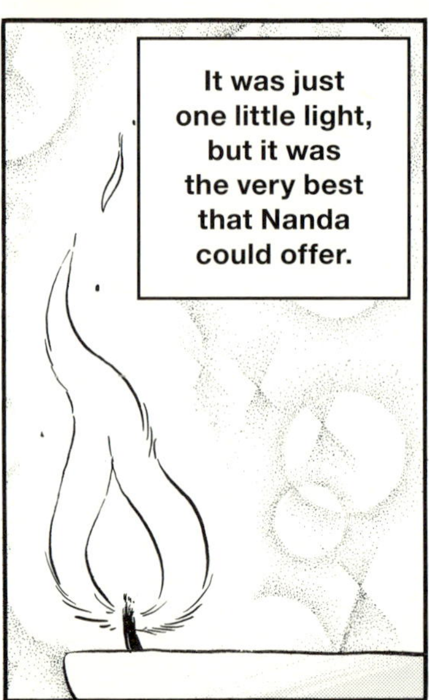
It was just
one little light,
but it was
the very best
that Nanda
could offer.

Of all the
thousands of
lamps there,
hers burned
the brightest.

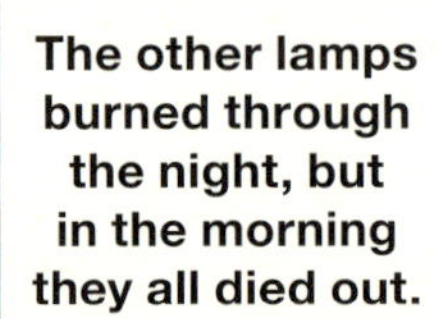
The other lamps
burned through
the night, but
in the morning
they all died out.

Only Nanda's
light kept
shining.
?
Buddha's disciple
Maudgalyayana
tried to put it out,
but he couldn't.

Lord Buddha,
what could be
the meaning
of this?

You lack the
power to
extinguish
that candle.

You might pour
the waters
of the seven seas
on it, and
still it would
burn on.

That is because
it was the
sincere donation
of a poor woman
named Nanda.
In the midst
of her poverty,
she offered
her very best.

From this story
comes the saying,
"A poor person's
one light
outshines
a millionaire's
10,000"!

The merit of giving
does not depend
on the amount
you offer.
What matters
is what's
in your heart.
Got it!

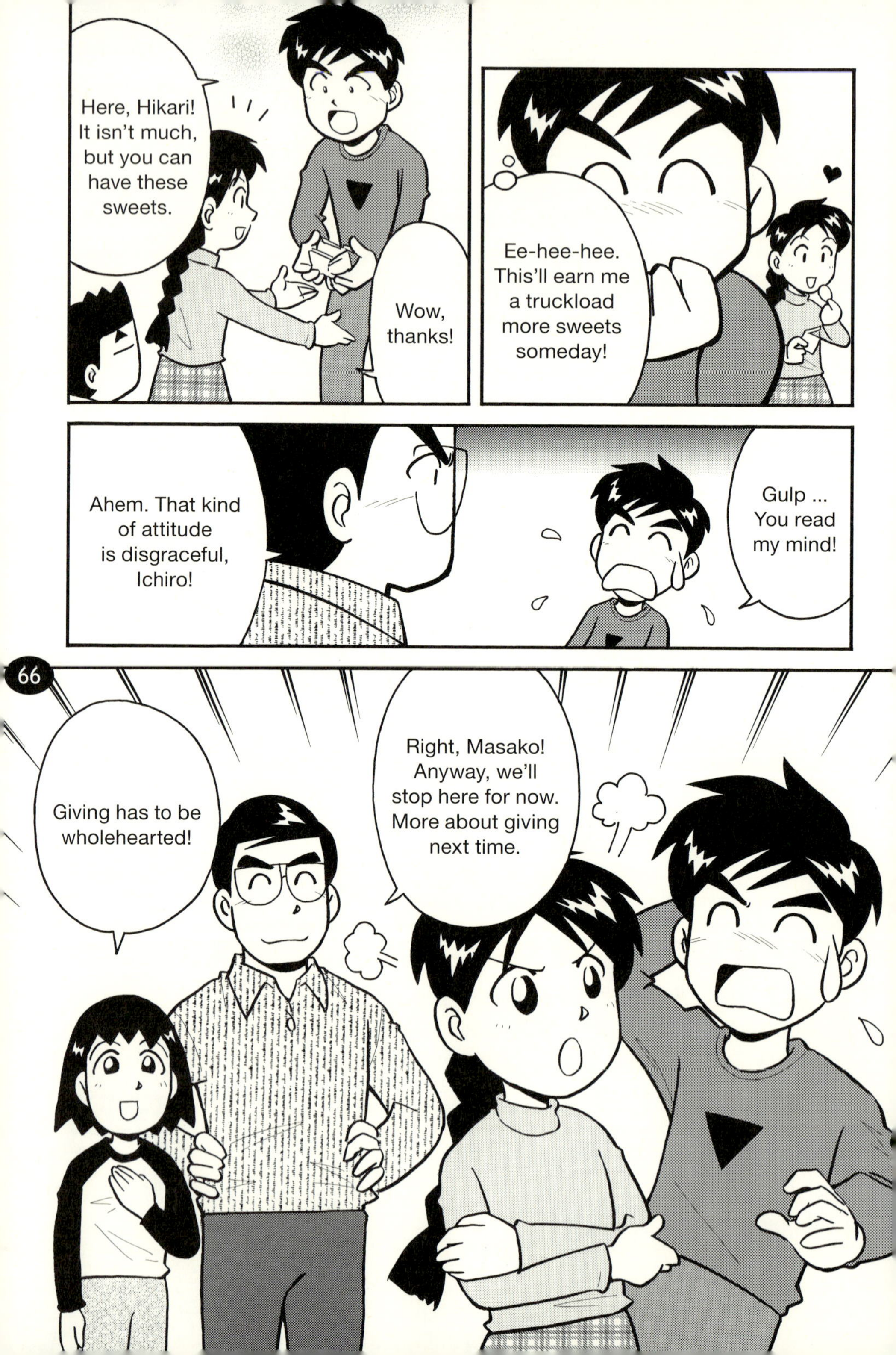

Right, Masako! Anyway, we'll stop here for now. More about giving next time.

Giving has to be wholehearted!

Lesson 8 **Six Good Deeds (3):**
Giving 2—The Seven Types of Nonmaterial Giving

Even if you have no money or possessions to give, you can still be generous.

* A place to hear Buddhist sermons

You what?
You want to
buy my land?
Yes,
Your Highness.
To build a vihara,
a place where
people can hear
Buddha preach.

No. It's not
for sale.
Please
reconsider ...

Your
High-
ness!!
Boohoo!
Tears
won't
move
me.

YOUR
HIGH-
NESS!!!
GRR!
Threats
won't
budge
me.

Princey-
wincey ...
Yikes!
The charm
treatment
won't work
either!
Agghh, get
off me!

All right, then!
If you want
that land, first
cover it in gold!
I'll trade you
the land
for the gold.

Really?!
Thank you,
thank you!

DASH
I'll do it
right away.
H-hey!

He'll never
come up with
that kind of
money.
flop

Go see what
he's up to!
Yes,
Your
Highness.

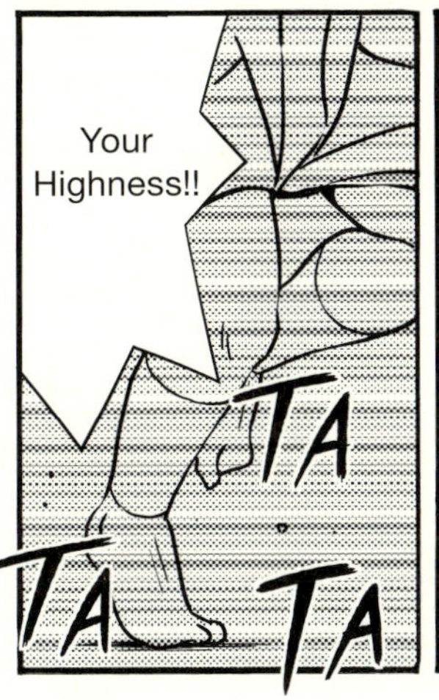
Your
Highness!!
TA
TA
TA

He's really
covering
the land
in gold!
WHAT?!

gallop

glitter
Aah, it's true! He's already half done!

W-wait! The depth of your regard for Buddha amazes me.

Let me contribute the remaining half as an act of giving.

And so Prince Jeta contributed the remainder. This became the famous monastery, Jetavana.
What an amazing story!

Oh yeah?
Mm-hmmm!
If it were me, and I were super-rich, I'd make donations all the time!

In any case, what should someone materially deprived, like me, do?

Use more kid-friendly words!!
eek!
Right. How scary ...

I mean, I have nothing. How can someone like me give anything to anybody?
A fair question.

You should know that in giving, what counts most is what's in your heart.

So even if you don't own anything, you can still give.
Really?

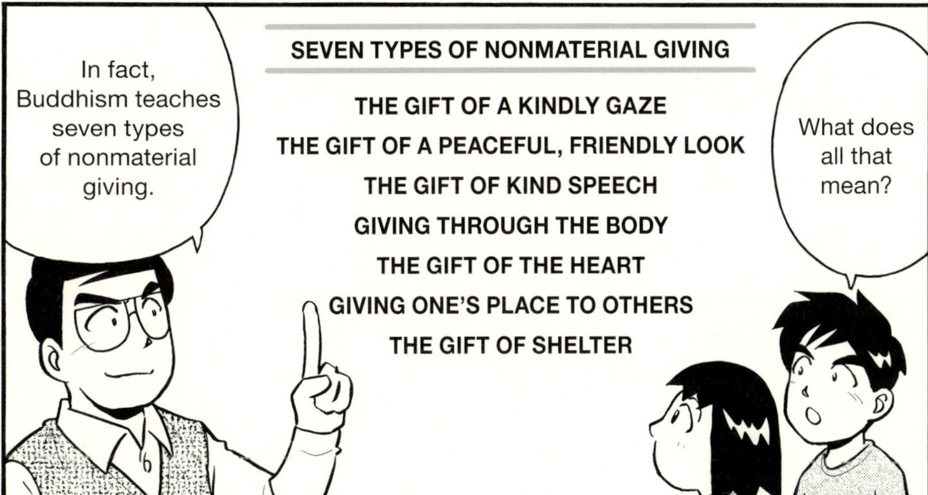
In fact, Buddhism teaches seven types of nonmaterial giving.
SEVEN TYPES OF NONMATERIAL GIVING
THE GIFT OF A KINDLY GAZE
THE GIFT OF A PEACEFUL, FRIENDLY LOOK
THE GIFT OF KIND SPEECH
GIVING THROUGH THE BODY
THE GIFT OF THE HEART
GIVING ONE'S PLACE TO OTHERS
THE GIFT OF SHELTER
What does all that mean?

THE GIFT OF
A KINDLY GAZE
Well, "the gift of a kindly gaze" means having a warm, gentle look in your eyes.
Huh. Can that be an act of giving?

Oh, right.

See? A kind look lifts the spirits of people around you and comforts people who are feeling down.
Ah, I feel better!

THE GIFT OF
A PEACEFUL,
FRIENDLY LOOK
"The gift of a peaceful, friendly look" means simply smiling.

Greeting others with a gentle smile is a wonderful form of giving!

THE GIFT OF KIND SPEECH

GIVING THROUGH THE BODY
"Giving through the body" means doing physical labor for others or for society.
SAFETY FIRST
All right! I'll take on any muscle job!
Smile ¥0
Then rub my shoulders and back for me.
Uh, sure ...

74

THE GIFT OF THE HEART
"The gift of the heart" means saying heartfelt thanks.
Ah, right there! Wonderful. Thanks a lot!
It's nothing ...
knead knead

"Giving one's place to others" means kindly giving up your place or seat.
GIVING ONE'S PLACE TO OTHERS
I always give my seat to old people on the train and bus!

Hee-hee.
But when it comes to food, Ichiro, you push people out of the way!
I've cut the cake!
WHIZ
The biggest piece is mine!
W-well ...

It's not just giving up your seat, Ichiro! We should always think of others first.

THE GIFT OF SHELTER
Finally, "the gift of shelter" means kindly granting a visitor or needy person shelter and a meal.

And that's all of the Seven Types of Nonmaterial Giving.
Got it!

They're all things that any of us can do anywhere and anytime, as long as we have the intention!

Remember the law of cause and effect: Good causes, good results; bad causes, bad results; own causes, own results.

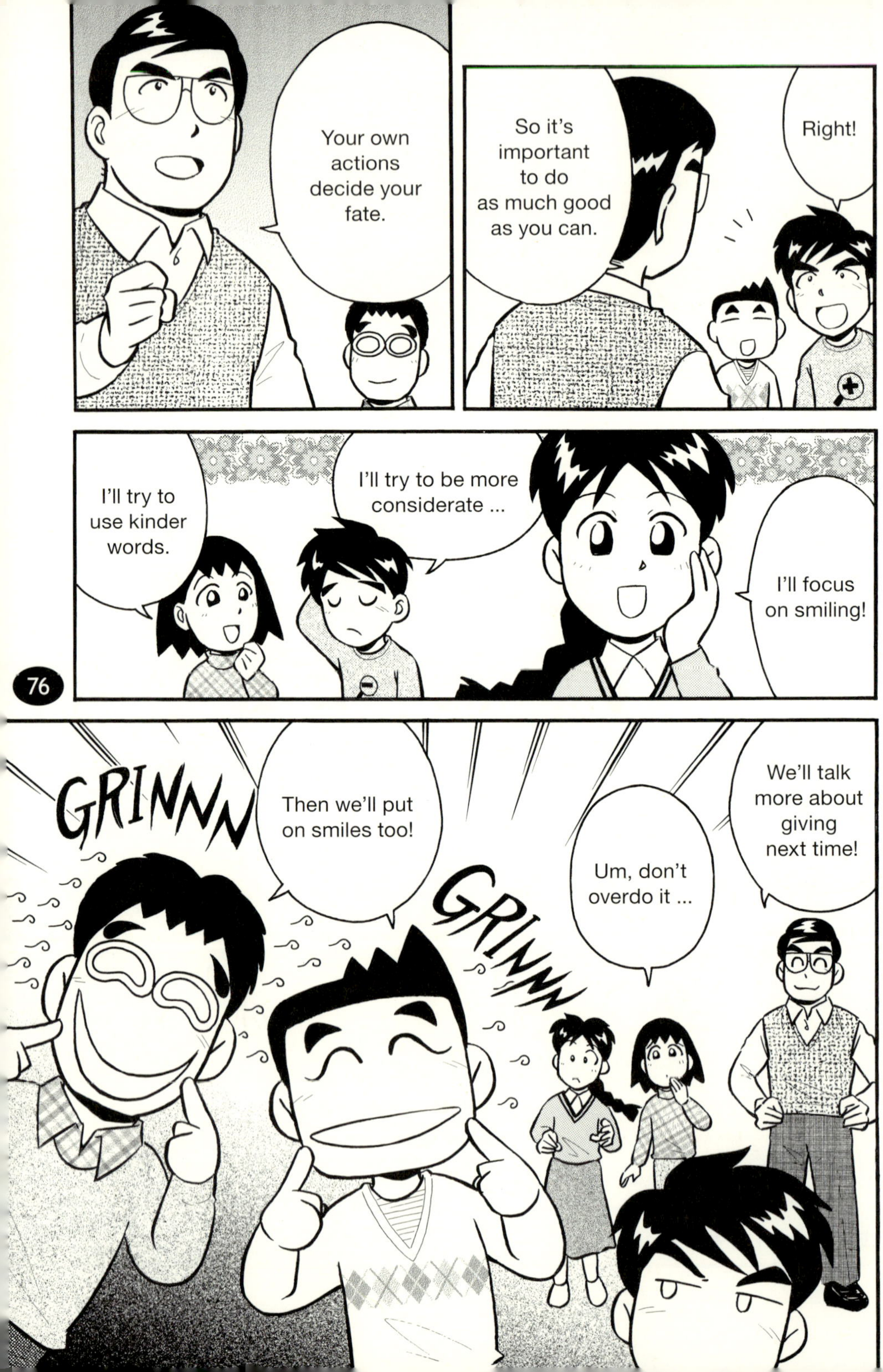

GRINNN
Then we'll put on smiles too!
GRINNN
Um, don't overdo it ...
We'll talk more about giving next time!

Lesson 9
Six Good Deeds (4): Giving 3—The Three Fields

Choose the objects of your acts of giving.

Oh, no?
Think about it. Helping a bad person allows him to go on doing bad deeds.

However kind your intentions, helping a thief is wrong.
Gee, thanks!
Allow me!

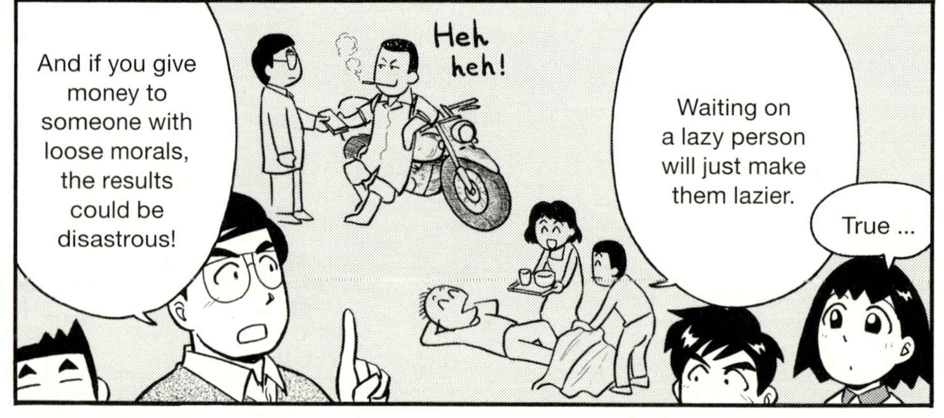
And if you give money to someone with loose morals, the results could be disastrous!
Heh heh!
Waiting on a lazy person will just make them lazier.
True ...

78

So you see, when you do acts of giving, you have to think about WHO you're helping, the recipient of your offering.

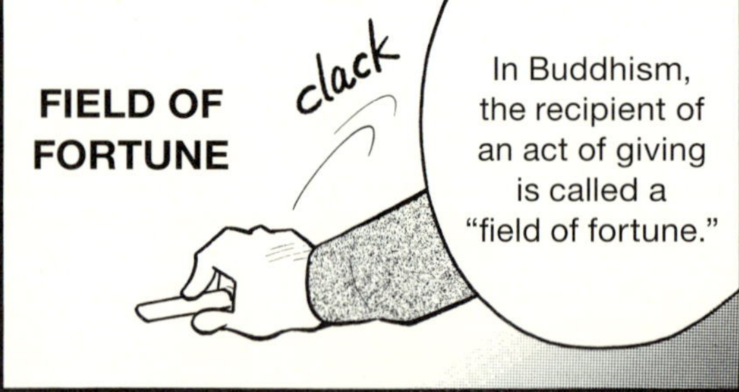
In Buddhism, the recipient of an act of giving is called a "field of fortune."
clack
FIELD OF FORTUNE

No, "field of fortune."
Wheel of Fortune?

It means a field where good fortune grows.

In the same way, if we practice sincere acts of giving, we will definitely reap good results.

Plant seeds in a field and a crop will soon grow, ripening into life-sustaining food.

So that's where the expression "field of fortune" comes from!
Right! A farmer planting seeds might think he's lost something because he gave up his seeds, but at harvest time he gets them back many times over!
A

No, "three fields."
Free fields?

FIELD OF RESPECT
FIELD OF GRATITUDE
FIELD OF COMPASSION
Buddha taught that there are three fields of fortune.
These are called the "three fields."

FIELD OF RESPECT
First, the "field of respect" refers to people who have virtue that should be respected.
FIELD OF GRATITUDE
The "field of gratitude" refers to people to whom we owe a debt of gratitude.

All of us are on the receiving end of kindness from all sorts of people!

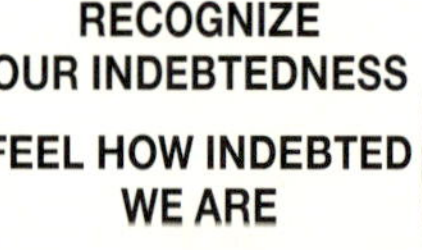
RECOGNIZE OUR INDEBTEDNESS
FEEL HOW INDEBTED WE ARE
TRY TO REPAY OUR INDEBTEDNESS
Buddhism teaches us it's important to recognize our indebtedness, to feel how indebted we are, and to try to repay our indebtedness.

That means to notice, appreciate, and try to give back for others' kindness, doesn't it?

Right! Try to think about who you owe a debt of gratitude to.
Umm ...

First is the debt of gratitude we owe towards Buddha and the teachers who convey Buddhism to us.

And
as you know,
you owe a lot
to your
parents!

They gave me
life and have
taken care of
me all this
time!
Yes
indeed!

Try to pay back
those you owe
so much,
in a spirit
of gratitude.

You yourself
will definitely
benefit!
Yup!

FIELD OF
COMPASSION
Last is
the "field of
compassion"—
people who
deserve our
sympathy.

People who
are suffering,
like disaster
victims
and the sick.
cough
splutter

It's important
to help those who
are suffering
and in distress.
We must do all we can
to extend charity
to them.

Now do you understand who you should be kind to?

Yes! I'll try to be more generous!
Hmm ...

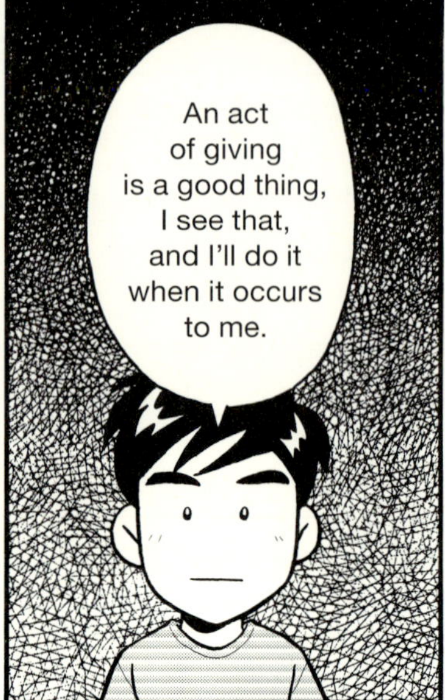
An act of giving is a good thing, I see that, and I'll do it when it occurs to me.

But first I need a nap to build up my energy!
flop
What's with those two?

Mm. Understanding the value of giving doesn't make it easy to do.

Huh.
It's because we're full of desires, wanting to sleep or have fun ...

Here's a story that Buddha told about someone just like that.

Hmm ...
What can I
serve?
Once upon a time, a man decided to invite a lot of people to a party.

I have
a cow,
so I could
serve milk!

MOO
But one cow
can't supply
enough milk
for them all ...
sigh

Ugh!
MILK
If I milk
the cow and
store the milk,
it'll go bad ...

I know!
I'll keep
the milk
INSIDE
the cow
till I need it!

I'm a
genius!
Um,
hey...

Soon the big day came, and all the guests arrived.
Welcome,
everybody!
buzz
buzz

I'll be right back with some fresh milk! Just a moment!
tmp tmp

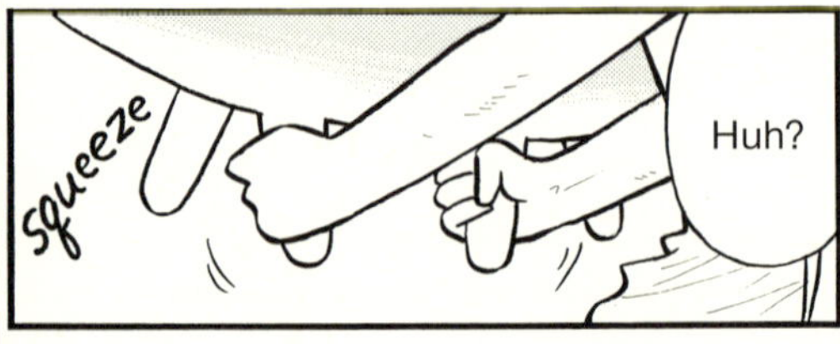
squeeze
Huh?

Weird. Nothing's coming out ...

The cow's milk had completely dried up. Not a drop came out.
What's going on?
Um ...

After the man confessed what had happened, his guests went home, disgusted and jeering.

After telling this story, Buddha explained, "I often hear people say they will do plenty of giving when they are better off ...
... but such people are like the man in the story. Giving is impossible for them."

So instead of putting it off, we should do good deeds right away!

He woke up!
Ta-da!
Like they say, "Hurry to do good"!

Remember the two types of giving? All of our discussion so far has been about material giving.
GIVING
DHARMA GIVING
MATERIAL GIVING

Now what would "Dharma Giving" mean, do you think?
Giving Buddhist teachings ... ?

That's right! It means to share Buddhism.

It means conveying Buddhist truth accurately to other people.
Can I do that???

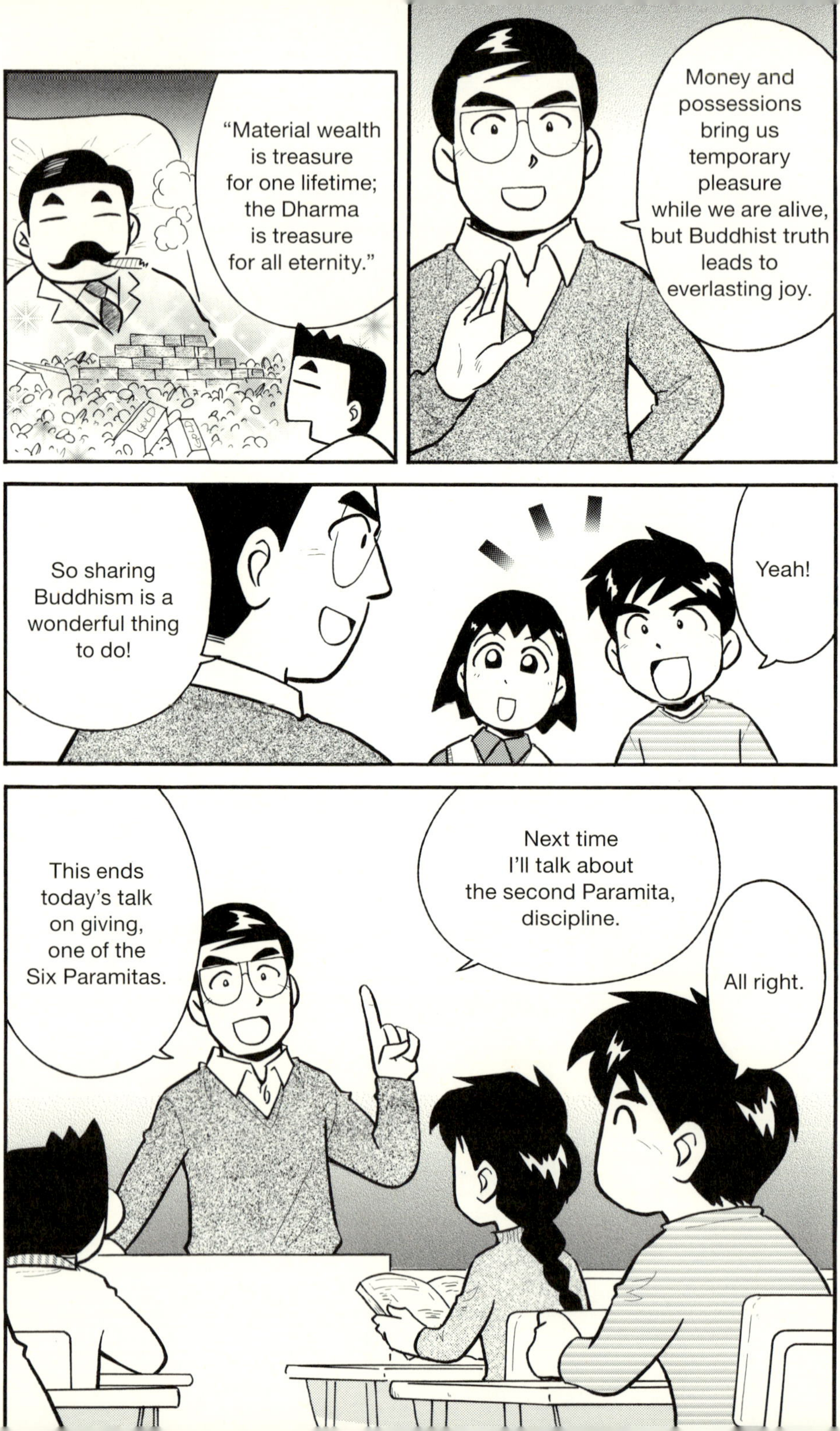

This ends today's talk on giving, one of the Six Paramitas.

Next time I'll talk about the second Paramita, discipline.

All right.

mutter mutter

Aw man, cleaning up is such a pain ...

Lesson 10 **Six Good Deeds (5): Keeping Promises and Patience**

Always keep your promises, and keep your temper, too.

Just because no one's looking doesn't mean you can slack off!

I-I'm sorry!
.com

Did you learn your lesson, Ichiro?
What do YOU want? Leave me alone!
.com

Hm. This seems like a good time to continue our discussion of the Six Paramitas.

chak
Last time was about giving.
That's right!

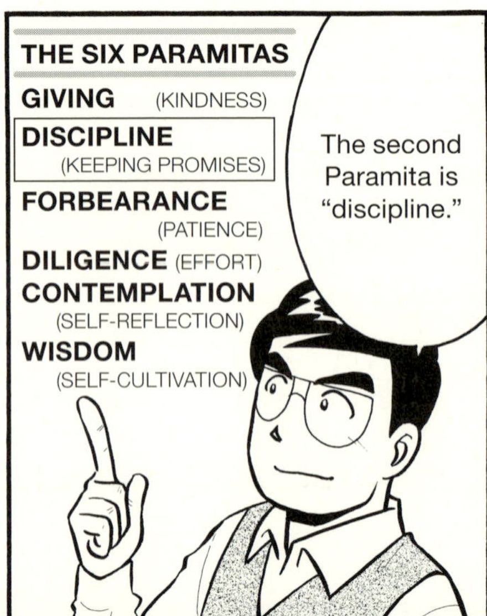
THE SIX PARAMITAS
GIVING (KINDNESS)
DISCIPLINE (KEEPING PROMISES)
FORBEARANCE (PATIENCE)
DILIGENCE (EFFORT)
CONTEMPLATION (SELF-REFLECTION)
WISDOM (SELF-CULTIVATION)
The second Paramita is "discipline."

"Discipline" means moderating what you say and do.
Moderating?
.com

In other words, avoiding saying or doing bad things.

Another way to put it could be "making your deeds match your words."

You mean always doing what you say you'll do?
Yes!

Always keep your promises. We're taught that's very important.

Doing what Ichiro did—offering to clean up, then walking off when no one's looking ...
.com

Being two-faced is sad, don't you think?
Urk ...
.com

Ichiro, have you learned your lesson??
Yeah, but ...

Listen. Even when you think no one's looking, a certain someone is.

No excuses, now!
Ooh, scary!
BONNNG

Gyah! W-who?
Buddha.

Buddha?!
Yes. He is all-seeing, all-hearing, all-knowing.

He sees everything we do ...
... hears everything we say ...
... knows everything that's in our hearts. Nothing is hidden from him.

Buddha knows, Ichiro!
H-he does?

With Buddha always at your side, moderate what you say and do. This is very important!

I'll tell you a story.
Once upon a time in Germany ...

... late at night when no one was looking, the king put a big stone in the town crossroads.

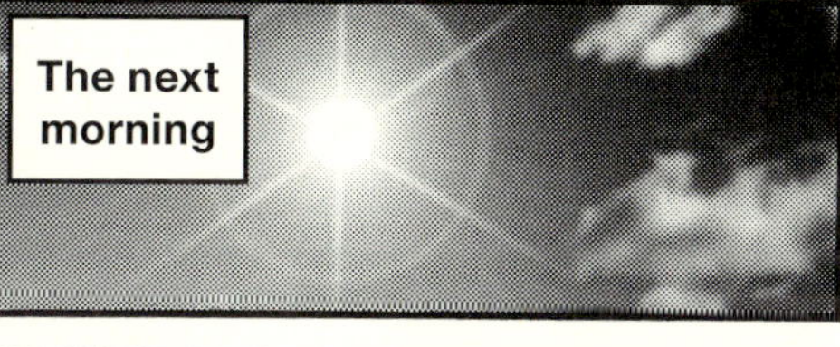
The next morning

trot trot

91

WHOA!
TSCHHH
That was close! I could have had a bad fall!

What a nasty prank.
Hmph!

clatter

Mm?

What the heck?! Who put a great big stone here ... I can't get by!

Stupid stone!
BOINK

clatter
hic

Whoo, I'm drunk!
hic

KERSPLAT

Owww!
Who put this friggin' shtone in the middle of the shtreet?

Sheesh, of all the *#%&! ...
mutter

A month went by, and no one ever tried to remove the stone.
Finally the king assembled the townspeople.
I am the one who put the stone here!

What a shame that none of you thought to move it for the sake of all ...

Now allow me to do so.

When the king moved the stone, there underneath it was a bag marked "Property of whoever removes the stone."
The bag was filled with gems and gold coins.

I'd have done it without being asked!

Good deeds yield good results, bad deeds yield bad results, own deeds yield own results. We've talked a lot about this law of cause and effect, right?

Erk ...
Right—for the sake of the gold!

If you do good things, good results happen. Bad deeds cause a bad fate!

And the deeds you do bring results for you yourself, right?
You've got it!

So it's important to moderate what you say and do, and be conscientious—whether or not anyone is watching!

If you do, you are sure to reap good results in the end.

Ichiro, are you listening?
Get off my back, will you!!!

Watch it!
Don't go flying off the handle!
.com
squirm kick
The third of the Six Paramitas is "forbearance"!

FORBEARANCE
"Forbearance"?
Being patient, putting up with things.

Anger
The opposite of patience is anger.

Anger makes us think terrible thoughts and do violent things.

Afterwards we're sorry, and wish we hadn't gotten so riled up ...
Argh!
Ugh!

The thing to do is step back and ask what made you so angry.
Anger evaporates as quickly as it flares up.

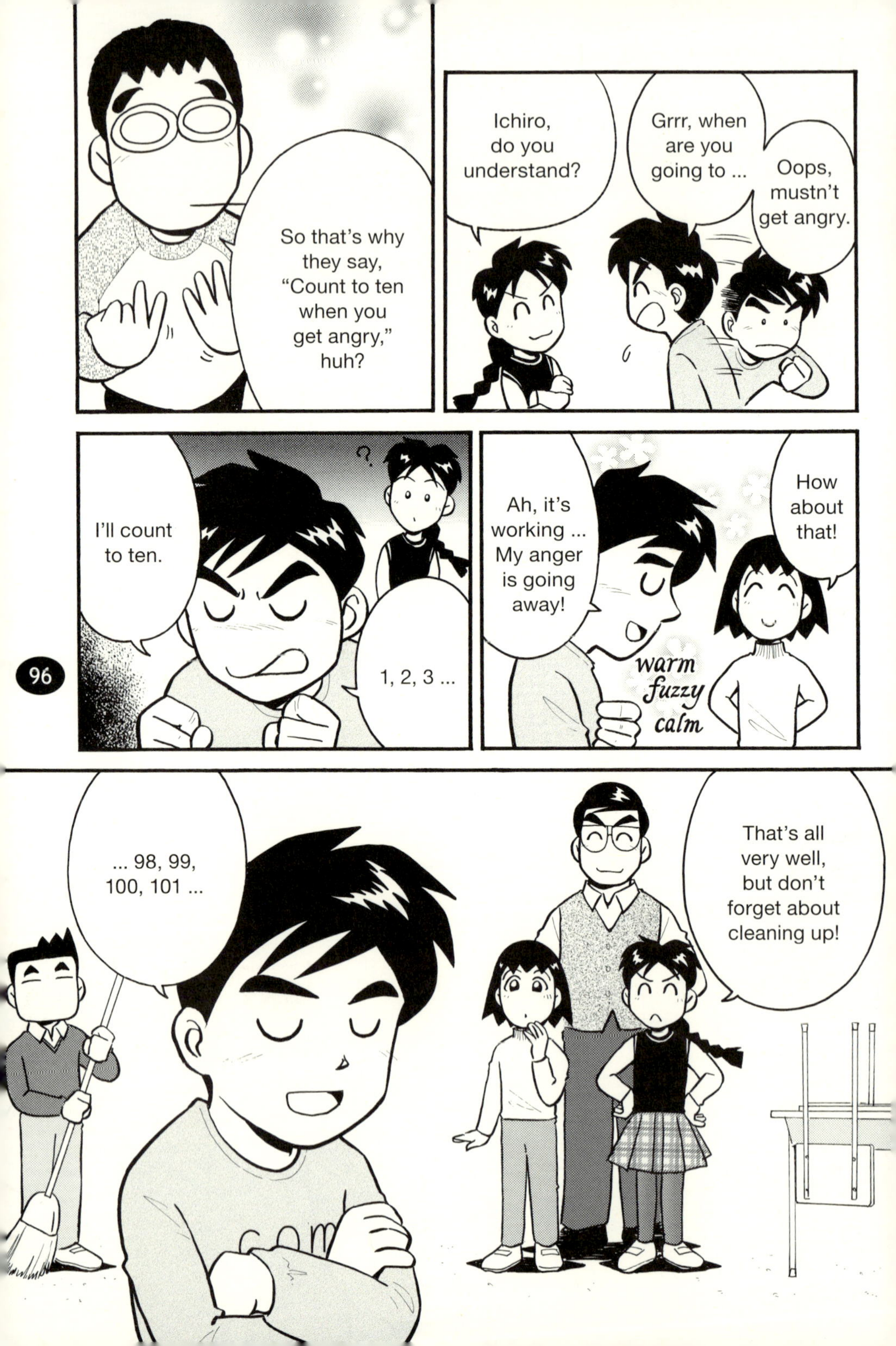

So that's why they say, "Count to ten when you get angry," huh?

... 98, 99, 100, 101 ...

That's all very well, but don't forget about cleaning up!

Lesson 11

Six Good Deeds (6):

Effort, Self-Reflection, and Self-Cultivation

Persevere—try harder than anyone else.

?
Shojin cuisine?

It is fresh! *Shojin* cuisine is dear to the hearts of Japanese people! It'll never go out of style!
mix mix

Seems old-fashioned. Why not something newer and fresher?

You don't know?
Whatever. What the heck is it, anyway?

Funerals?
Shojin cuisine is traditionally served at Buddhist memorials and funerals.
Simmered veggies, sesame tofu ...

Right! It's really nutritious, based on soy products and vegetables.

It's vegetarian. No meat or fish.

So the word *"shojin"* means not eating meat or fish?
Hmm, maybe so.

Well, a lot of people think so, but actually that's not the real meaning.

Oh, Mr. Suzuki!
Where are we ???
This is a perfect chance to continue our talk on the Six Paramitas.

I remember! Buddha summed up all possible good deeds in those six, right?

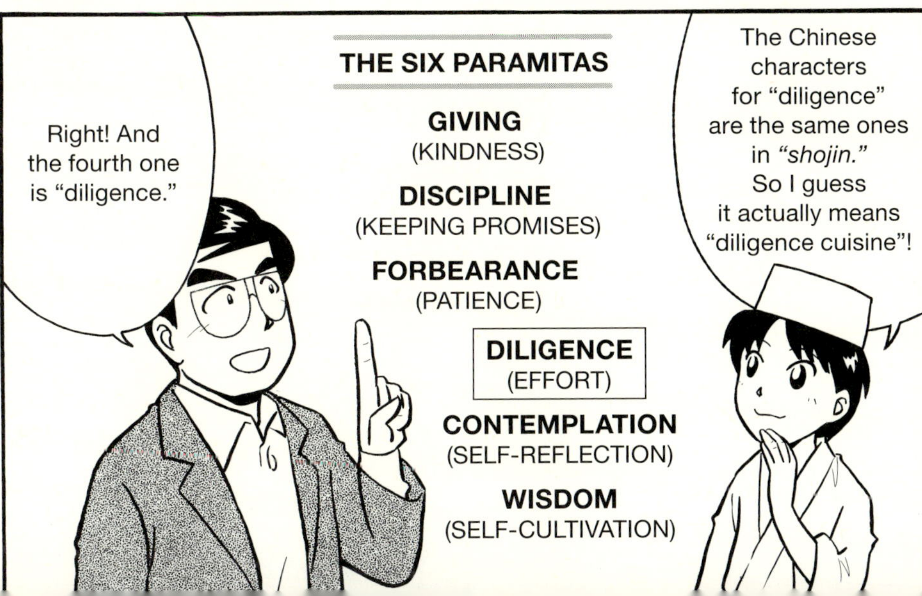
Right! And the fourth one is "diligence."
THE SIX PARAMITAS
GIVING (KINDNESS)
DISCIPLINE (KEEPING PROMISES)
FORBEARANCE (PATIENCE)
DILIGENCE (EFFORT)
CONTEMPLATION (SELF-REFLECTION)
WISDOM (SELF-CULTIVATION)
The Chinese characters for "diligence" are the same ones in *"shojin."* So I guess it actually means "diligence cuisine"!

And "diligence" means putting in effort.

Hmm ...
It's got nothing to do with food then ...

Mind you, to be diligent it doesn't matter if you eat vegetables or meat or anything else!

What matters isn't what you eat but whether you make an effort.
Makes sense!

I wanna stuff myself on roast beef and lie around doing nothing!
That's disgusting!

We're all like that. We do as we please, and hope for good results ...

Let me tell you a story.
Long ago, two peddlers always crossed a high mountain pass.

Huff,
puff ...

Man,
this is
rough!

If only the pass
weren't so high,
we could cross it
easily and make
more money ...

So said the
first man's
companion.
I have to
disagree.

I say just
the opposite.
It'd be better
if the pass
were higher
yet!

Do you
WANT to
go through
hardship?!
Are you nuts?

If we could
cross over
easily, so could
our competition.
We'd make
LESS money,
not more.

102

But if the pass were higher and steeper, NO ONE else would cross it!
We'd do a rip-roaring trade!

See, if you put in ordinary effort, your results will be just ordinary, too.

People who are successful really do think on a different plane.
Hmm...

I once heard you only get two things by taking it easy: poverty and shame!

Aha.
Diligently going to extra trouble is the way to get great results!

Really?
Yes. It's the same with cooking.

It takes long, hard training to create dishes that people ooh and ah over!
CHOP STIR

Here you go!
SWOOSH
Oh, wow!

Looks great!
Mm? A bit salty, isn't it?

WHAT?! You've got a lot of nerve, buster!!
Come on now, relax!
Eck!
WHAP

Quiet your mind. Try to understand why this happened.

CONTEMPLATION
(SELF-REFLECTION)
The fifth of the Six Paramitas, "contemplation," means self-reflection.

"Self ... reflection"?
Yes. While your mind is upset, you can't judge things correctly.

It's important to calm down and reflect carefully on yourself.

Actually maybe I did measure wrong ...

Oh!
I won't make the same mistake again!

That's the ticket! Now you can make progress!

The last of the Six Paramitas, "wisdom," means looking clearly at the law of cause and effect and improving yourself. It sums up the other five.

Thank you, Mr. Suzuki!
Now we've covered all of the Six Paramitas!

Giving, discipline, forbearance, diligence, contemplation, wisdom.
Can you name all six?

Good for you, Ichiro! To sum up:

People who are kind to others and keep their promises ...

... who exert themselves and make extra efforts ...

... and who reflect on their actions, are certain to succeed.

People who are unkind, who say one thing and do another, break their promises ...

... blow up easily and do only what they want ...

... and never reflect on their actions—they haven't got a chance of success.

Oh!

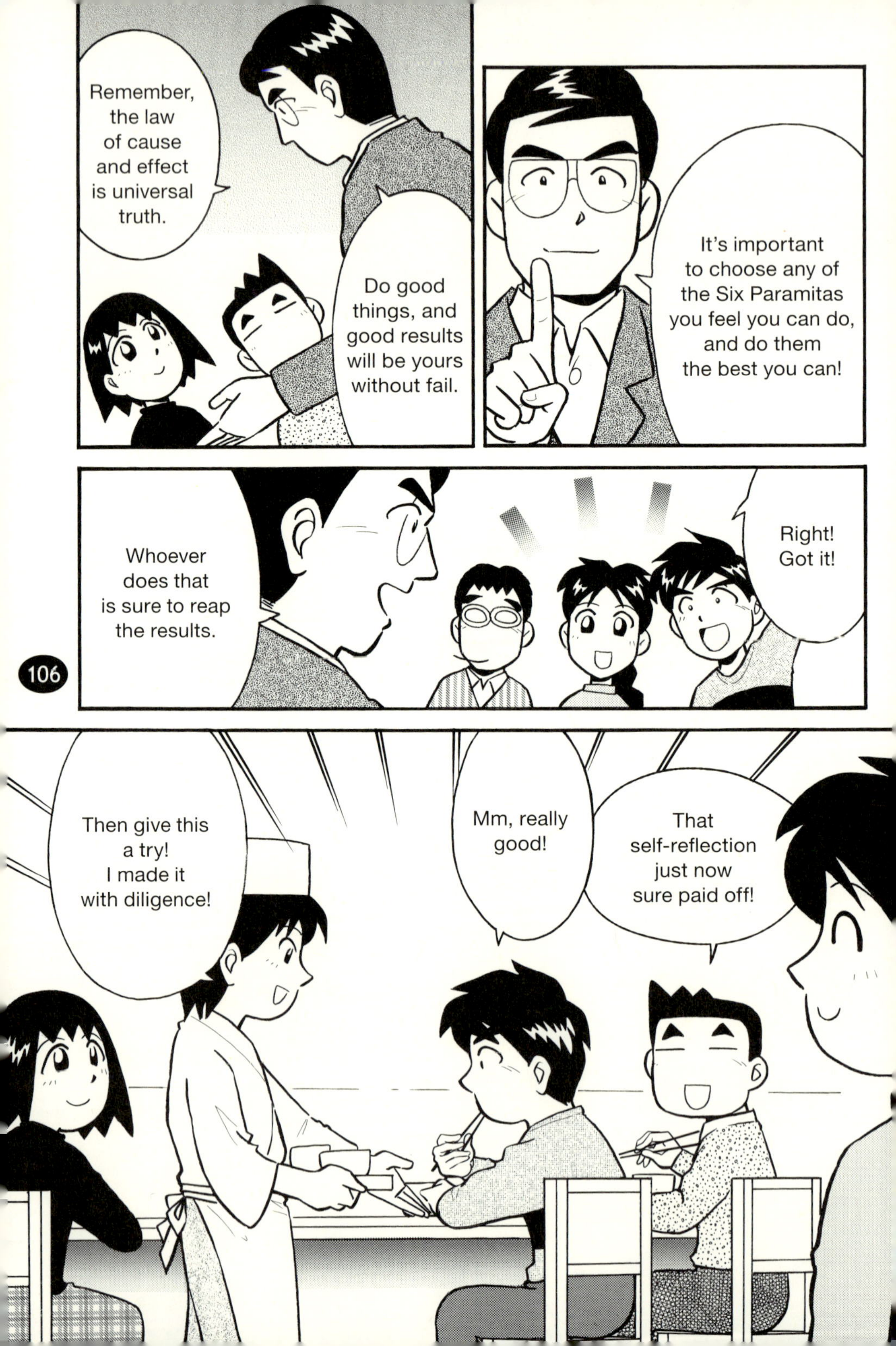

Then give this a try! I made it with diligence!

Mm, really good!

That self-reflection just now sure paid off!

Lesson 12

The Flower Festival — Buddha's Birthday

The real meaning of "Only I am holy"

This is my present.
RUSTLE
Oh, my!

Look at all the pretty flowers! They're lovely.

Heh heh. After all, today is the Flower Festival.

No, "flower" as in "pretty plant"!
"Flour" as in "baking cookies"?

Heh heh.
Hmm, was there a festival like that?

April 8 is Hikari's birthday, but surprise—it's Buddha's birthday, too!

Ahem. Yes.
Who knew?
Buddha's birthday?

Yup, on April 8 about 2,600 years ago, he was born in a flower garden called Lumbini Park.
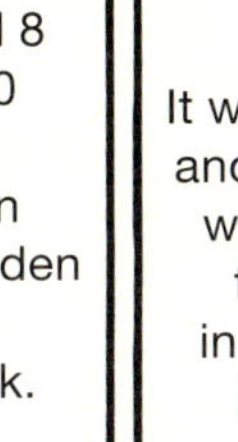

For once Naoki is running the show.

It was spring, and the park was full of flowers in glorious bloom!

That's why people came to celebrate Buddha's birthday with a Flower Festival.
Huh.

Now we know what the Flower Festival is! That's it for today.
FWUP

109

Time for cake!
Good grief. All you think about is food.

Wait, I just remembered.
?
BAP

Right after he was born, didn't Buddha say something?

Try to remember!
What was it ... ?

Anyway, I'm having my cake!
yum
CAN

He said, "In heaven and earth, only I am holy."

Not again! He's always popping out of the woodwork ...
GUAHH!
Mr. Suzuki!
CAN
THUMP THUMP

No way! Newborn babies can't talk ...
It's true, they do say that when Buddha was born he pointed upward and then downward and said those words.

Mm. That may be true.

Still, the words contain an important meaning that we need to pay attention to.

Let's see. He said, "In heaven and earth, only I am holy."
In heaven and earth, only I am holy.

So he was saying that the greatest, holiest person in the world was him.

111

Sheesh! So full of himself!
Wait, don't be too sure.

A lot of people take it that way. They think it just sounds conceited.

But actually he didn't say it to show how great he thinks he is. It means something else.

There's a saying, "The mature rice plant lowers its head."

Right.
bow
Truly great people act humble and respectful.

Hmm ...
If that's true for ordinary people, it's even truer for Buddha!

So what did he really mean?

Listen. The words "in heaven and earth" refer to the vastness of the universe!

ONLY
"Only" means "just." Only one.

112

I
The next word, "I," doesn't refer to the Buddha alone.

It means each one of us!
Oh.

And the last word, "holy," means a "single sacred mission."
HOLY

So he's definitely NOT saying that he's the only person who's great.
Ah.

What it really means is this: "In the vast universe, we humans ...
... are born into this world with a single sacred mission to perform."

What's a mission again?

We've heard before that "a single human life outweighs the earth."
Life ...
Its kanji character is like this shape!

A mission is what you devote your life to.

Easy! Making gobs of money!
KA-CHING
KA-CHING

Hmm. What could you devote your life to so you'd feel that kind of joy?

For me, winning the Nobel Prize and gaining fame and status ...
Mm.
Clap
Clap

Finding and marrying the woman of my dreams!
Ha-ha-ha-ha!

Money and possessions, fame and status— those are all important things in life.

We strive so hard to get them. But the point is, why must we keep living ...
... even through such struggles? This is the most important issue, is it not?

Why do we live ... ?

You mean the ultimate purpose of life?
Yes.

Achieving life's purpose so that we can obtain the joy that shouts "I'm glad I was born human!" ... THIS is our sacred mission.
I see.

Buddha clearly laid out the purpose of human life.
Sakyamuni

So let's use Buddha's birthday as a chance to study Buddhism carefully.

OK!

Who knew that April 8 was such an important day?!

Now let's get back to Hikari's birthday party!

POP

Huh? The cake's all gone!

Awol!

I celebrated all by myself!

I'll whip up another cake!

BURRRP

It's not your birthday, it's mine! Give it back!

Lesson 13
The Eight Sufferings (1)

Birth, aging, sickness, and death are inescapable.

Now that you mention it ...
He must have gotten separated.

I THOUGHT it was awfully quiet ...
Haha!

Hey! Wait up!
There he is.

I was looking around, and before I knew it I lost the trail!

wheeze
gasp
What happened? Where've you been?

That's dangerous! Don't go off by yourself.
S-sorry.

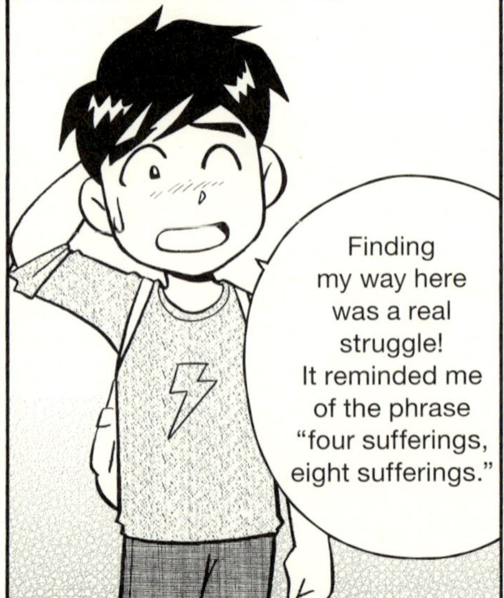
Finding my way here was a real struggle! It reminded me of the phrase "four sufferings, eight sufferings."

Hey, that's a Buddhist expression. Do you know what it really means?

Um, I guess you use it to talk about having a hard time?

It's used for any struggle, isn't it? Like studying for a big test?
Hm.

It was Sakyamuni Buddha who taught this. It expresses the suffering we all go through in life.

"Suffering ... in life"?

You say that like it's got nothing to do with you!
Lay off!

Four hundred years ago, the shogun Tokugawa Ieyasu said, "Life is like traveling a long road, laden with a heavy burden."

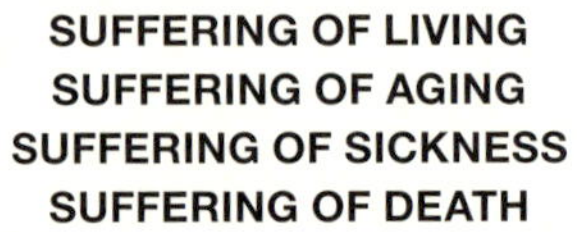

SUFFERING OF LIVING
SUFFERING OF AGING
SUFFERING OF SICKNESS
SUFFERING OF DEATH

THE FOUR SUFFERINGS

SUFFERING OF SEPARATION FROM THE BELOVED
SUFFERING OF ENCOUNTERING THE DESPISED
SUFFERING OF NOT GAINING WHAT ONE SEEKS
SUFFERING OF BEING OF THE FLESH

EIGHT SUFFERINGS IN ALL

THE SUFFERING OF LIVING
First is the suffering of living itself.

Entering this world through birth is itself a form of suffering.
Hmm ...

All the suffering we experience wouldn't have happened if we'd never been born!
True.

From children to adults, everybody is suffering.

I want to stay in bed, but I have to go to school every day!

Life is sooo hard!
Now, now!

THE SUFFERING OF AGING
Next is the suffering of aging.

As we get older, our eyes start to go, we get wrinkles, our hair gets thinner, and our bodies don't work the way they used to.

If only my face could remain unchanged as the years pile on, though life must end.
This poem was written by Ono no Komachi, a great beauty of ages past!

It means "I want to keep my looks, even if my life has to end."

Not even the greatest beauty of all time can defy age.

She must really have suffered.
Wha?
Mm-hm.

No beauty salons in those days!

Ewww! I don't want to get old and ugly!!!
Um, you're still in grade school ...

THE SUFFERING OF SICKNESS

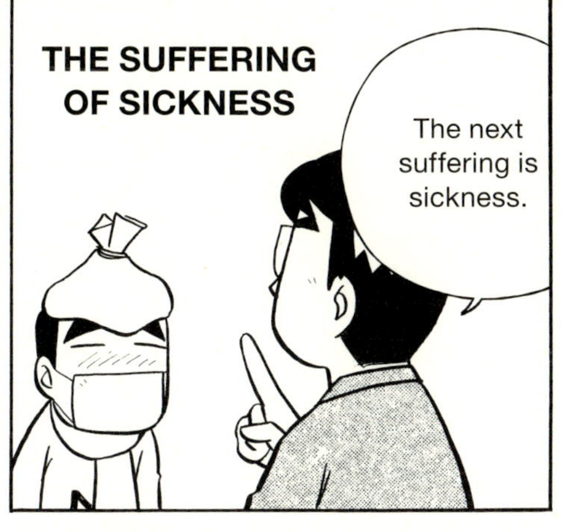

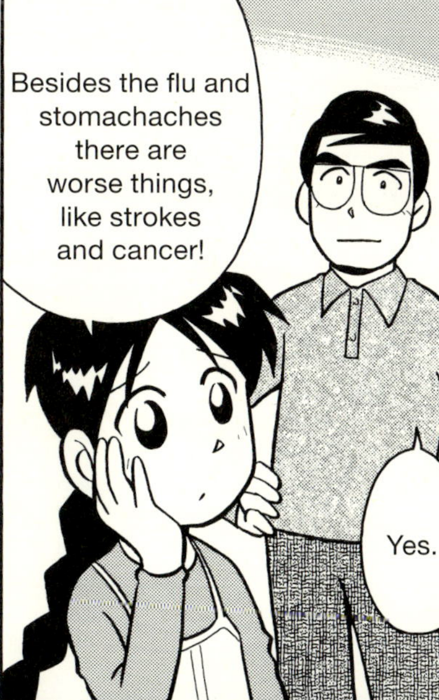

But even if it's just a headache, everyone thinks their own pain is worst of all.

It's hard to say what suffering is lesser or greater.

Nothing is so awful as a stomach-ache!

Medical science can't abolish sickness.
Yeah.

A tooth-ache is the worst pain EVER!
BZZZ
Don't cry!

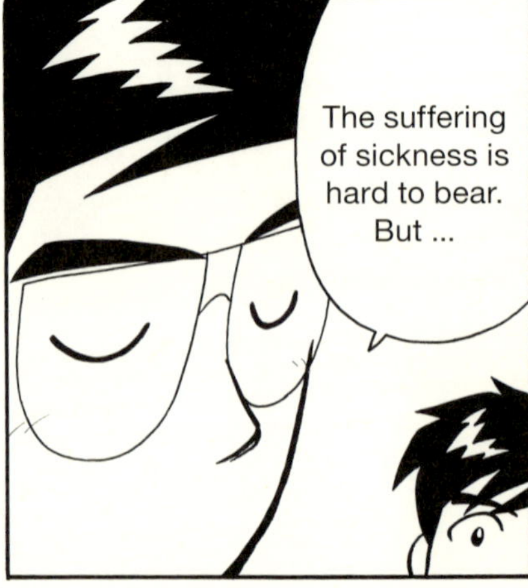
The suffering of sickness is hard to bear. But ...

The greatest suffering of all is death: Everyone has to die one day.

THE SUFFERING OF DEATH
However happy you may be, death destroys all your happiness in an instant.

In Japan, the number four sounds like "death," so hospitals don't use it!
Huh?

There are some flowers whose names contain the sound for "death" in Japanese.

They are considered unlucky.

Gahh, get those flowers out of here!
Oops.

Just the sound of the word "death" makes me feel sad.
Mm-hmm.

That's because we have an instinctive fear of death.

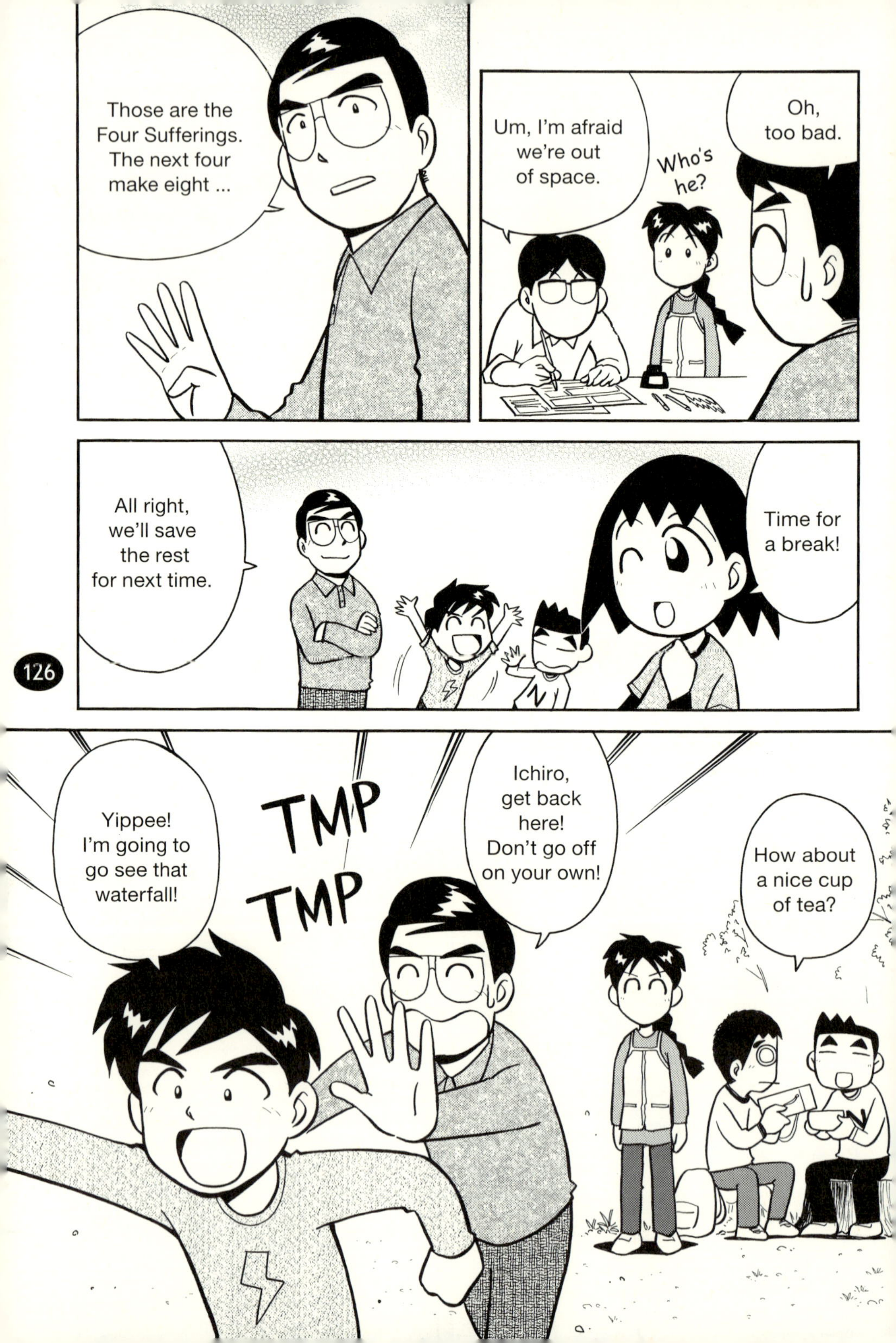

Yippee! I'm going to go see that waterfall!

TMP TMP

Ichiro, get back here! Don't go off on your own!

How about a nice cup of tea?

Lesson 14
The Eight Sufferings (2)

A world overflowing with love and hate

You get hungry because you're always running off on your own!

Mmf!

Oh, the pain ...
hufff
pufff
Sheesh, look at him!

All right, let's have an early lunch!

Yay! Lunch! Lunch!
FWUP

But wait. First, let's talk about what we learned last time.

Huh?
Forgot already? "Four sufferings, eight sufferings," remember?

Er, OF COURSE I remember!
Yeah, right.

Buddha divided the suffering we all go through in life into eight kinds.

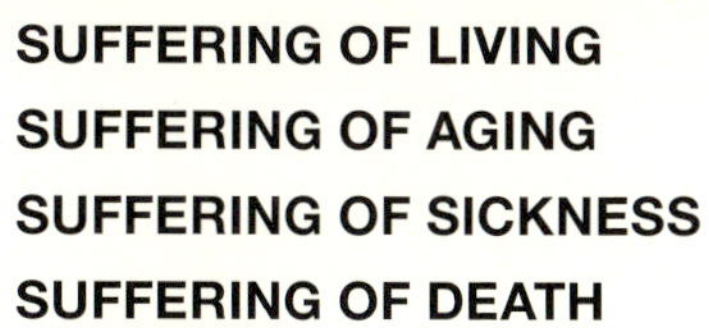
SUFFERING OF LIVING
SUFFERING OF AGING
SUFFERING OF SICKNESS
SUFFERING OF DEATH

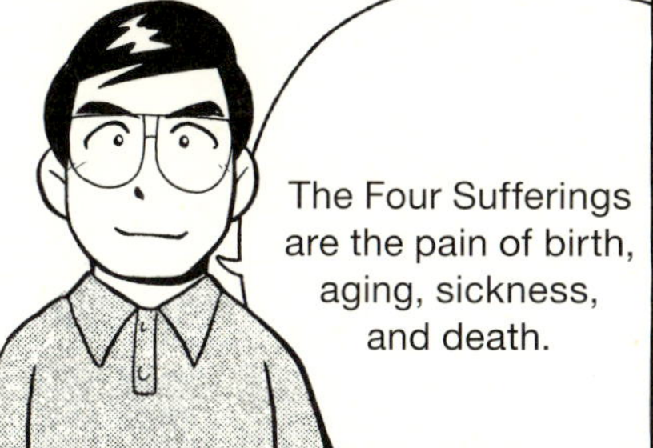
The Four Sufferings are the pain of birth, aging, sickness, and death.

SUFFERING OF SEPARATION FROM THE BELOVED
SUFFERING OF ENCOUNTERING THE DESPISED
SUFFERING OF NOT GAINING WHAT ONE SEEKS
SUFFERING OF BEING OF THE FLESH
And there are four more, for a total of eight.

Last time we studied the first four.

This time we'll take up the remainder.
OK!

SUFFERING OF SEPARATION FROM THE BELOVED
First is the suffering of having to part from people and things you love.

You and I were meant for each other!
Lovey
dovey

Sh-she dumped me!
BOO HOO!
FSHHH
One way or another, it happens. Parting is inevitable, in life or in death.

My best friend is moving away! I can't bear it!

My pet hamster died. It's so sad.

Mm. One thing you can be sure of: No matter how much you love someone or something, in the end you must part.

Like they say, "Meeting is the beginning of parting"! It's true, huh ...

SUFFERING OF ENCOUNTERING THE DESPISED
There's the opposite kind of suffering, too—having to encounter people or things you hate.

Sometimes there are classmates you just can't get along with.
I hate bullies!

WOOF WOOF!
GRRR!
That dog always barks— I don't like it!

Somebody's stalking me! I'm scared!
Uh-oh!

The teacher always gives us homework, and we can't escape him!
Ssh!

SUFFERING OF NOT GAINING WHAT ONE SEEKS
Ahem. Number seven is the suffering of not being able to get what you want. For example, money, possessions, status ...
WHOA!

LOVE
I want a girlfriend!!!
QUEST!

This makes the 20th time he's been dumped!

No matter how I try, I can't hit the ball like Ichiro does in the major leagues!
BLIP
BLIP
PAF
Um, you're playing a video game ...

Argh, I want the latest game console!!!

Absolutely not! This old one of your father's is good enough.

Not gaining what you seek, huh?
B-but it's 20 years old!!

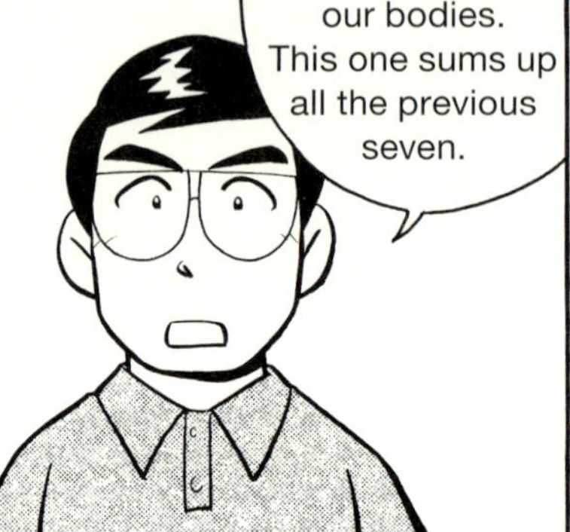
SUFFERING OF BEING OF THE FLESH
The last one means sufferings inherent in our flesh—suffering that comes because we have our bodies. This one sums up all the previous seven.

Gosh, life is pretty heavy going.

It's hard to see the point of being born at all.
You're right.

Oh ...
When you take a good look at life, you can't help feeling that way.

But NOBODY was born just to suffer.

Buddha taught that all human beings can attain true happiness. He said that our lives have an ultimate purpose, and that when we attain it, we will know vast satisfaction and rejoice that we were born.

I'd love to be happy like that!
Yes indeed!

So let's keep on studying Buddhism!

Hip hip hooray!
Okay—so now I know all about the Eight Sufferings.

That means it's time to chow down!
Typical, typical ...

My lunch is sashimi, raw fish!
That might not be safe to eat. You'll get sick.

I brought a nice big roast beef sandwich ...

RUSTLE

It's gone! It's not in my knapsack!

Oh look, there's a hole!

NOOOO! It must have torn on a tree branch.

That's what happens when you go off by yourself. Honestly ...

Gotta find it!!

What if a badger is eating it right now?

He wants to eat but he can't—he's not gaining what he seeks!

Ughhh...

Lesson 15
The Blind Passions

Why are temple bells struck 108 times on New Year's Eve?

Agh, the more I remember, the more frustrated I feel!
DONNNG
DONNNG
DONNNG
Take that ... and that ... Auggh!

Hang on, you're losing it!

WHEEZE WHEEZE
You OK? Calm down!

What came over me?
Are you positive that's how to ring in the new year?

What do you do this for anyway?
Ahem. I'll explain.

On New Year's Eve it's customary for temple bells to be struck 108 times.

The number 108 represents the number of blind passions, right?

Yes. Buddhism teaches that "blind passions" are what trouble and torment us, and we each have 108!

Oh really?
On New Year's Eve the bell is struck to banish the blind passions that caused such trouble all year, so the coming year will be peaceful!
NAGOYA

DONNNG
There!
Well, that explains why he was remembering all that stuff.

Sorry about that!

Wait, didn't you do this last New Year's Eve, too?

Year in and year out, you make the same wish!
Um ...

The blind passions don't vanish. You never make a dent in them!

Erk!
No progress.

Mr. Suzuki!
The thing is, we are made of blind passions!

HA HA HA!
All right, you!

138

Yes.
Nothing but blind passions?

Buddhism teaches that human beings consist of nothing but blind passions.

Think of a snowman. Take away the snow and what do you have?
roll roll

In the same way, take away our blind passions and nothing is left.

What the heck is a "blind passion"?
Oh really?
NAGOYA

And what are the 108, exactly?

OK. Of the 108 blind passions, three are especially dreadful.

139

DESIRE
ANGER
IGNORANCE
They are desire, anger, and ignorance.
These are called the "three poisonous passions."

That's right.
"Three poisons"?

munch munch
“Desire” is the longing for something. If you don’t have it, you want it. If you do have it, you want more and more without end.

“Anger” means getting mad.
KABOOM

“Ignorance” leads us to blame and resent others: “It's all his fault!”

I see!

Let's talk about the first one, desire.

Buddhism teaches that there are five typical desires.

Hmm.
What are they?

DESIRE FOR FOOD
DESIRE FOR WEALTH
DESIRE FOR LOVE
DESIRE FOR FAME
DESIRE FOR SLEEP
We desire food, wealth, love, fame, and sleep!

DESIRE FOR FOOD
The desire for food means the pleasure of eating.
CHOMP CHOMP
Bring on the goodies!
SLURP

TASTY TREATS
BURP
Sweets!
Gourmet foods are in style. Everybody likes to eat.
BLUB
BLUB

DESIRE FOR WEALTH
Desire for wealth means the pleasure of accumulating money.

I want to make money, I don't want to lose a cent.
KACHING
Money makes the world go'round!
KACHING

But drive farther and end up spending more on gas?
OGLE OGLE
I study the ads to find the cheapest bargains!
BARGAIN SALE
SALE

DESIRE FOR LOVE
Desire for love means the pleasure of intimate relations.
I have a crush on Takeshi!
Don't go!

Aren't there any cute girls around here somewhere?
How can you say that with me right in front of you?!
FWUP
FWUP

DESIRE FOR FAME
Desire for fame is the desire for praise and honor. We want to be admired.
CLAP
CLAP
CLAP

I want to be a world-famous Nobel laureate!
Ahem!
Forget it.

I'm hot, just ask anyone!

I'm getting beauty treatments. My goal is to be Miss Universe!
Cosmetic surgery, liposuction, botox—they're all popular.
Shine

DESIRE FOR SLEEP
Desire for sleep makes us want to rest and take it easy whenever possible!

Just a little longer ...
BAM
Come on! You'll be late for school!!

What do you say? We're at the mercy of these desires every day, aren't we?
It's really true.

Often we make trouble for others or cause them pain by trying to satisty our desires.

We need to do some soul-searching.
Yeah.

I spent too much time being lazy this year.
LAZE LAZE
Get up!

You goofed off and didn't do your homework.

We mustn't let our desires for food, sleep, and fun take over!

Let's look back and reflect on our behavior, and aim high in the year ahead!
NAGOYA
The bell-ringing is really about self-examination.
DONNNG
OK, I will!
How about some hot noodles?
Now you're talking!
The biggest bowl is for me.
Hey, no fair! I saw it first.
Looks like the blind passions are here to stay, all right ... !

Lesson 16

Abusive Talk, Words That Kill

We mustn't hurt others with our words.

She's so smart and sweet ...

TWINKLE
TWINKLE
Her smile is what really gets me.

Huh?
HA HA HA!

Eheee!
You don't know the real Hikari.

Um, really?
There's nothing sweet about her! She slugged me yesterday, good and hard.
SWIP
WA

She's bossy and lords it over me all the time.
WA

That's not what I'm saying!
You're that wimpy?
WA

Hikari's stupid and weird, and this, and that ...
CLENCH

Mm?
Just a minute! How can you say things like that!

Ah!
BAM
H-Hikari! I didn't see you!

Don't try to cover up. How dare you!

Ichiro has been acting terrible! He called me names!

Gyah!
YANK
It's unforgivable!

Oh, Mr. Suzuki!
W-what's all this?

What?
That's not nice, Ichiro.
C-come on!

A deed of the mouth?
Good cause, good effect.
Bad cause, bad effect.
Own cause, own effect.
A good deed makes a good result.
A bad deed makes a bad result.
You always reap what you sow.

What did I say that was so bad?

If you say something bad, later on you will definitely pay the consequences.

?
You don't get it, do you?
WA

149

Yes.
For example, "abusive talk."
ABUSIVE TALK

It does?
Listen.
Buddhism teaches all about the evil that comes out of the mouth.
WA

ABUSIVE
TALK
Abusive?
It means bad-mouthing somebody.

Saying negative things about someone or cursing them.

You might not even really mean them, but even so, words like these are hurtful and you must never say them.
I wish you were dead!
You stupid idiot!
You piece of trash!

150

Some people say nasty things about others behind their backs.
It's called backbiting.
Yikes!

And he was ...
When friends talk about someone who's not present, they're often critical. It's a bad habit we need to keep in check.

Think about it.
Haven't you all had your feelings hurt by criticism?

Now that you mention it ...
Mm-hmm.

Hurting someone with your words is a kind of murder.

Here's a story for you.

The murder weapon is words. You don't know it, but your words go on tormenting people till the day they die.

151

One day she had a visitor.
In your long life, you must have had many interesting experiences. Would you care to share your memories?

Once there was a woman who lived to be 120.

Plenty happened, all right, but the older I get the harder it is to remember.

She's 120 years old! It's understandable.

Still, there must be something you could tell me.
...

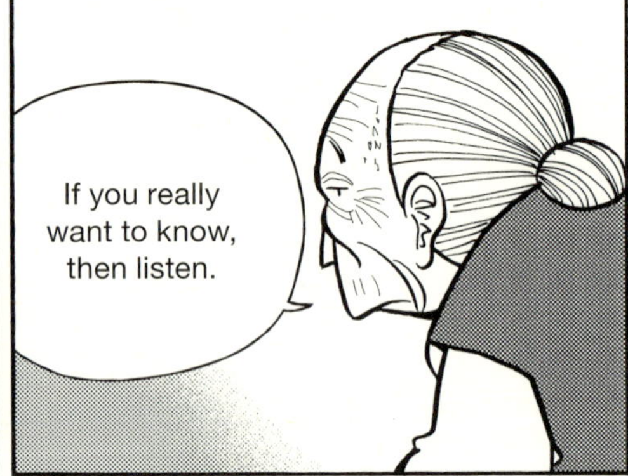
If you really want to know, then listen.

All I have is the memory of being killed 24 times.

Eh?

You're alive now, so how could you have been killed 24 times?

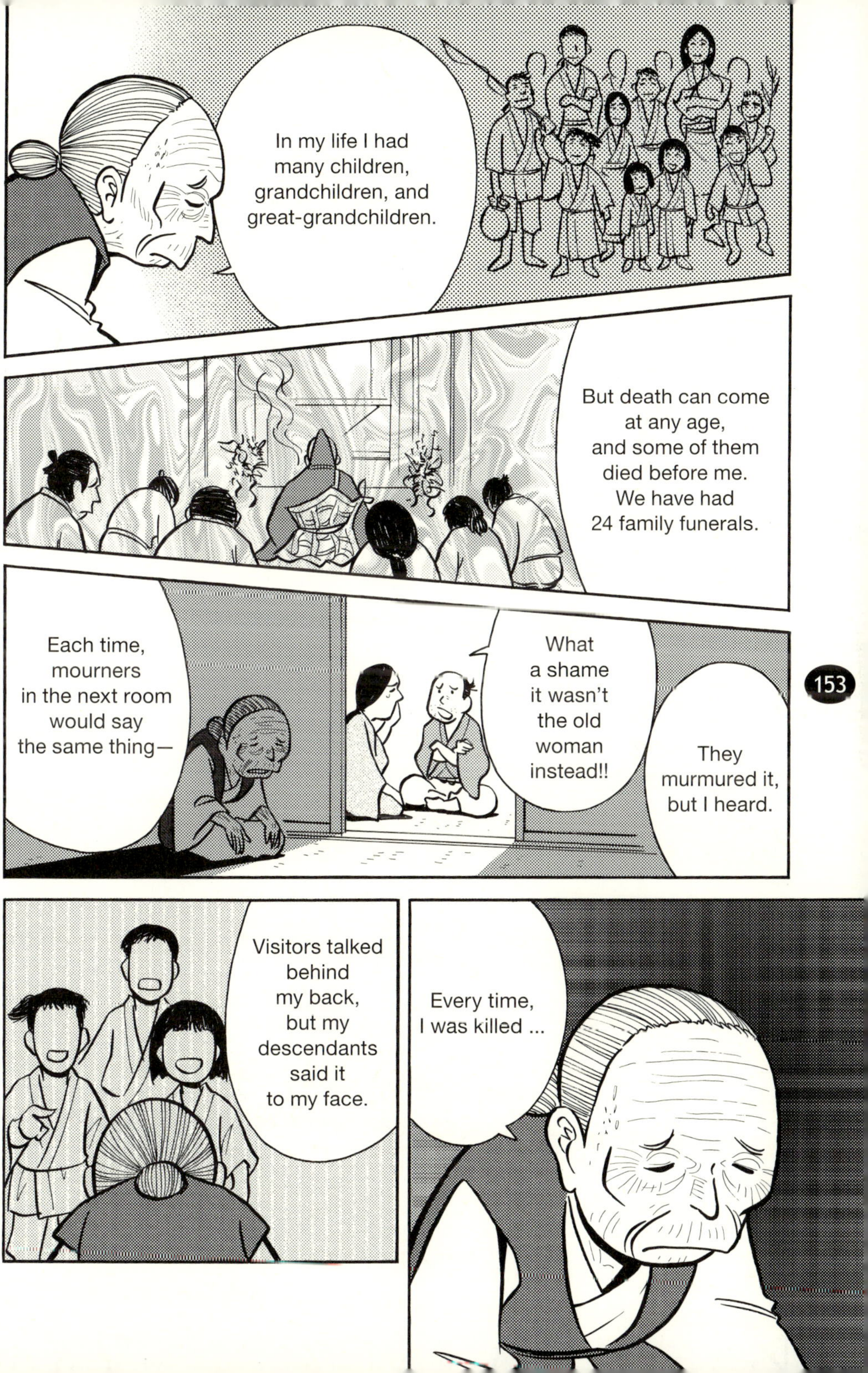

In my life I had many children, grandchildren, and great-grandchildren.

But death can come at any age, and some of them died before me. We have had 24 family funerals.

Each time, mourners in the next room would say the same thing—

What a shame it wasn't the old woman instead!!

They murmured it, but I heard.

These days, people think nothing of sending cruel text messages or of posting horrible things on the Internet!

...

That is not right. It's really sad.
Weirdo!
Wacko!
Die!

Not so good.

Think how you'd feel if someone said those words to you!

A junior high-school kid tried to kill himself because of cyberbullying.

In South Korea, malicious postings actually drove an actress and a singer to suicide.

This is what they call "verbal abuse," right?
Mm-hmm.

Even the most casual word has so much power to do harm, huh . . .

Even if no one knows what you did, you're bound to reap the consequences of your actions. Think it over!

Well!
Mr. Suzuki, I understand now. The things I said were terrible.

I won't do it anymore.
It's you yourself who'll suffer from what you said, you know.

It's not good to get carried away.

I wonder if he's really going to give her the letter?

WA

Lesson 17
Ignorance (Envy)

The ugly mind that begrudges others their happiness and takes pleasure in their misfortune

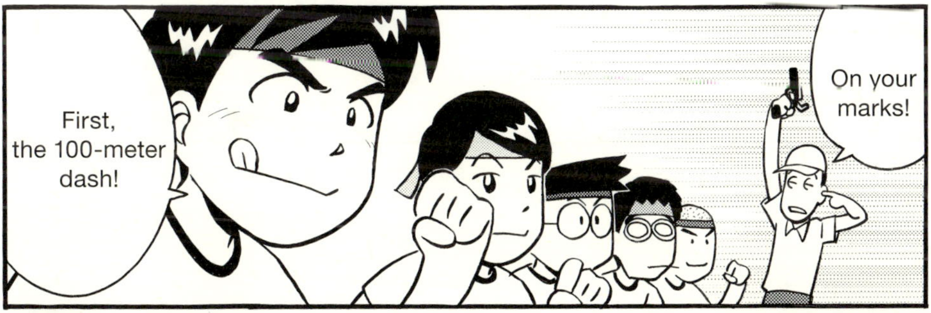

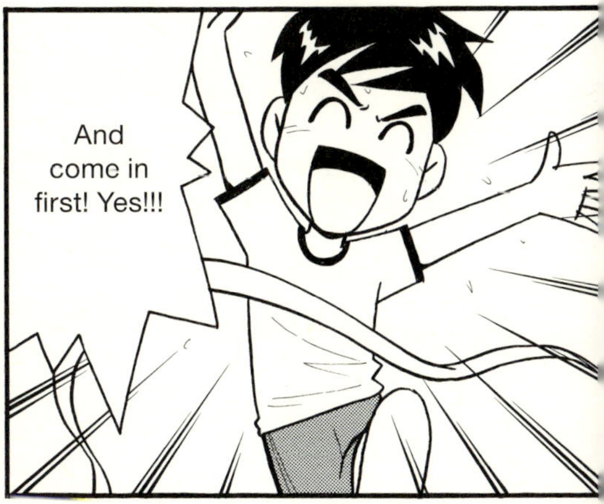

First, the 100-meter dash!

On your marks!

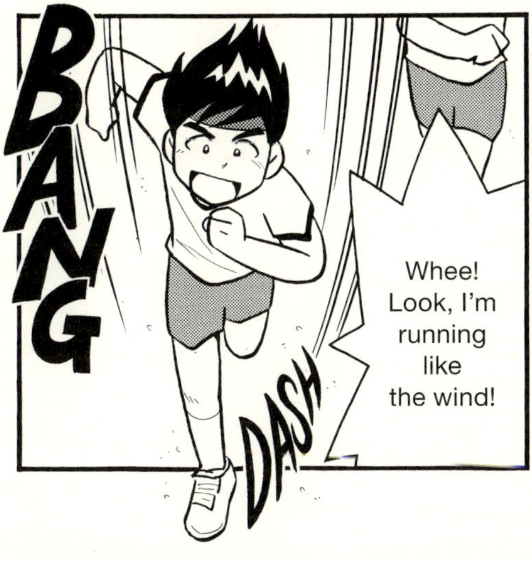

BANG

DASH

Whee! Look, I'm running like the wind!

And come in first! Yes!!!

TA-DAH
But no! Tatsuki came in first, Ichiro second.
What!! No way!

How could anybody outrun me, Ichiro?

There's always the next event.
Ruaagh!

BANG
OK, I'll definitely win the hurdles!

TA-DAH
Tatsuki, first place!

Next, the ball-rolling contest!
Next, the scavenger hunt race!
Tatsuki wins!
Next ...

Nobody's counting on you!
What's going on? People are counting on me to get a medal in the next Olympics ...
How can I lose so miserably?

Tatsuki, you came out of nowhere!
Heh heh!
1

Rats. After all the training I did to get ready!
poke
Um, did you??

I did my very best, so why did this have to happen?!!

He's grumbling because he lost.
May I say something?

Do you know the real reason why we grumble?

Grumbling comes from envying others' fortune and enjoying their misfortune.

In Buddhism, this is called "ignorance."
IGNORANCE

"Ignorance"?

Grumbling stems from the foolish mind that is ignorant of the law of cause and effect.

The law of cause and effect? We learned about that before!
Um, we did?

If you forgot, check out lesson 2!

That's right. Every effect has a cause.

There can't possibly be an effect without a cause.

Seeds not planted will never grow; seeds planted will never fail to grow.

THE LAW OF
CAUSE AND EFFECT
ACTION
A "cause" is an action, something we do.

Good actions bring good results, bad actions bring bad results. Our results always grow out of our own actions.

So happiness comes from sowing good seeds!

And unhappiness is the result of our own bad actions.

161

When good things happen, it's easy to be glad.

When bad things happen, we think, "How could this happen to me?!" We blame others, think the world is against us, and are consumed with envy.
Waahh...

See that? I won fair and square!

162

GAAAAAHH!!
My misery is all Tatsuki's doing! HE's the problem!!!

This happens because we don't grasp the law of cause and effect in a real sense.
Right.

Ulp!
I hear envy and bitterness! Oh, the horror!

Urgh!
Grr. I can't just shake it off!

I wish Tatsuki would fall and break a leg!
That's ignorance talking!

Resentment of excellence is a scary thing.

We don't like the sight of others' good fortune.
Sometimes we even wish disaster on them instead.
100
32

Agh!
ZHHH
Har
Eek!
SPLASH
And the sight of others' misfortune gives us pleasure.

It's really sad, huh.
All that comes from ignorance.

He's still at it.
Waaahh...
I'm trying so hard ... I did all I could, and what for ...

Yes. Well, Ichiro's feelings are understandable!

But it's important to ask yourself if you REALLY did all you could.

I practiced! I ran 100 meters twice after school!

That's it?
Every other day!

GOBBLE
For the rest, to keep up my strength I ate well and slept.
ZZZ

HUFF PUFF
I jogged two kilometers every morning and did stretching exercises. Every night I lifted weights and ran 10 laps.

See?
Um, what about you?
...

TA DAH
Oh, what a manly physique! It's blinding!
No waaay!

How old are you, really??
There you go. Everybody did reap as they sowed.

All right, I admit it. I didn't try hard enough.
You finally figured that out?
flop

Seeds sown will surely grow; seeds not sown will never grow. No effect can happen without a cause.

The next race is about to begin! Line up here!

Wait!!

DASH

Maybe this time Ichiro will make it ...

Lesson 18
Seven Kinds of Pride

Human beings can’t get away from conceit.

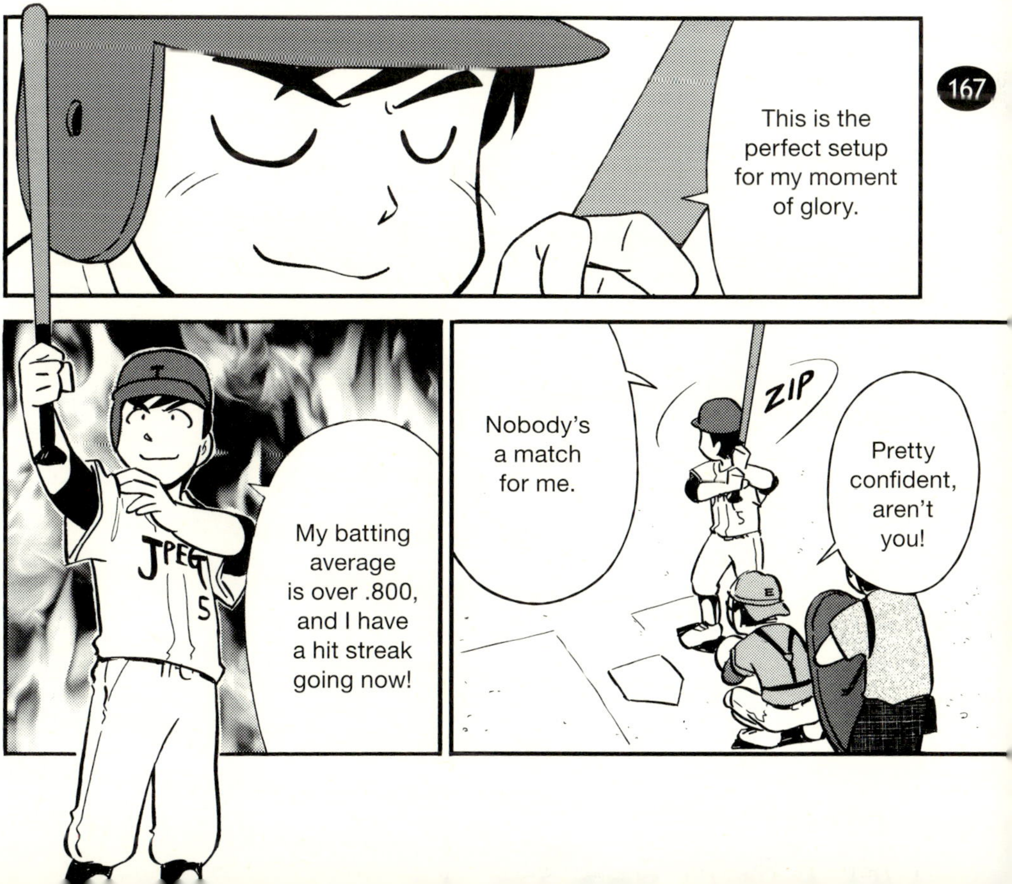

This is the perfect setup for my moment of glory.

My batting average is over .800, and I have a hit streak going now!

Nobody’s a match for me.

ZIP

Pretty confident, aren’t you!

Ichiro in the major leagues has got nothing on me!

The REAL Ichiro is standing right here! Bring it on, Tatsuki!
Unngh ...

Whaddaya mean? I'm just being honest!

Your ego is a bit out of control, isn't it?

I can hit any ball, anytime!

I can see it coming, and I'll knock it out of the park!
FWA

Good grief. Sounds like you're conceited to me.
Heh heh. You bet I can see it!

The blind passions are part of Buddhist teaching, right?

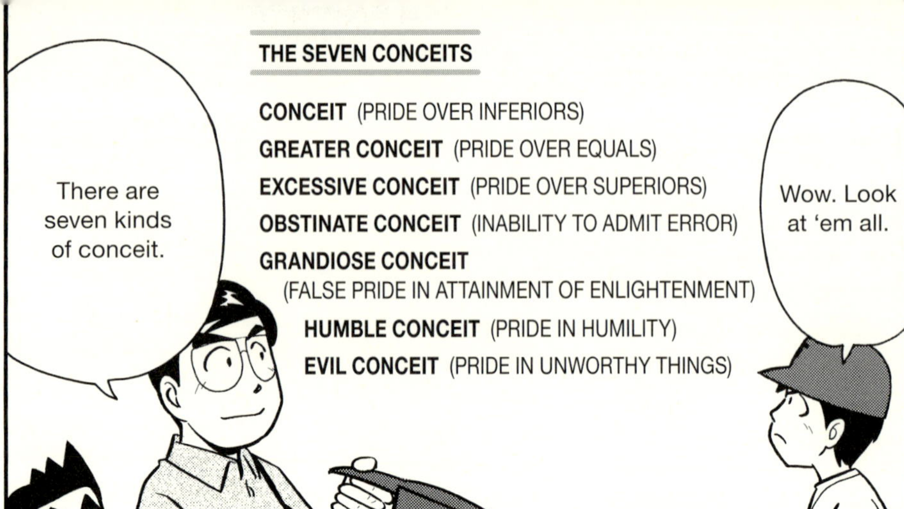
There are seven kinds of conceit.
THE SEVEN CONCEITS
CONCEIT (PRIDE OVER INFERIORS)
GREATER CONCEIT (PRIDE OVER EQUALS)
EXCESSIVE CONCEIT (PRIDE OVER SUPERIORS)
OBSTINATE CONCEIT (INABILITY TO ADMIT ERROR)
GRANDIOSE CONCEIT (FALSE PRIDE IN ATTAINMENT OF ENLIGHTENMENT)
HUMBLE CONCEIT (PRIDE IN HUMILITY)
EVIL CONCEIT (PRIDE IN UNWORTHY THINGS)
Wow. Look at 'em all.

Buddhism looks carefully at the human heart.

Buddha taught us all about what's really in our hearts.
Huh.

The first kind of pride means lording it over those inferior to you and looking down on them.
100
60
What the HECK are they doing?
Who knows?
Geez!

The next means lording it over those who are your equals.

Wait, what's that mean?
How can you be conceited when you're inferior?

The third one means thinking yourself superior to others even when you are their inferior.

Ok, here's an example. Ichiro, how did you do on the tests?

Math was hard, but I aced the English test!
A fluke ...
FLAP
100
JP
E
EPS

What? I'm smart and the test proves it!
I can't believe it!
Anyway, you did well.
5
E
EPS

By the way, Hikari aced that test, too.
100

Yeah, but—hee-hee—get this! The day before the test she studied like crazy!

She can't compete with me there!
Um ... shouldn't you compete against other boys?
THWACK

That's the third kind of conceit—thinking you're better than someone even though you're inferior.

What's that got to do with it! No matter what you say, I'm right!
He's being difficult.
THUNK THUNK

That's "obstinate conceit" (*gaman*) : refusing to admit you're wrong even though you know perfectly well that you are.

In general Japanese, the same word "*gaman*" is used to mean "endure," or "hang in there."
SIZZLE SIZZLE
It's so hot...
Bear up, Ichiro! Gaman!

The Buddhist meaning is completely different.
I did not know that.

GAAHHH! We are so full of conceit!

"Grandiose conceit" is thinking you have achieved enlightenment when you haven't.

The sixth kind is "humble conceit." Saying, "I still have a lot to learn," while actually thinking, "Gee, look how humble I am!"

A familiar kind of conceit.
How cool am I?
No one is as poor an excuse for a human being as me.
JPEG

"Evil conceit" means taking pride in something unworthy.

Like a thief priding himself on his stealth and quickness.
ZOOM
ZOOM
Look at me!

Really? I'm number one? Hurrah!
Ta-ha-ha!
Ichiro, you forget things more than anyone in our class!
JPEG

That's precisely what I'm talking about: pride in something unworthy.

Do you understand the seven kinds of conceit?

Buddha taught that all these forms of conceit exist in every human heart.
Really?

Yeah, I have to say they do in my case.
He finally gets it!

We can't ever get away from these seven kinds of conceit.
I see.

Now you understand.

Unless we listen to Buddhism, there is no way to know our own foolishness.

OK, back to the game. Play ball!
What were they doing all that time?
YEEEAH!
Wooooo!
Bring it on. I'll knock your fat pitch right out of the park!
Smartass!
Mmf!
SWOOSH
WOOOOOSH
Take that!

How could this happen to me! Agh!
Strike three! Yer out!
TOSS
See what happens when you get too cocky?

Lesson 19

Know Gratitude, Feel Gratitude, Show Gratitude

An ingrate is not to be trusted.

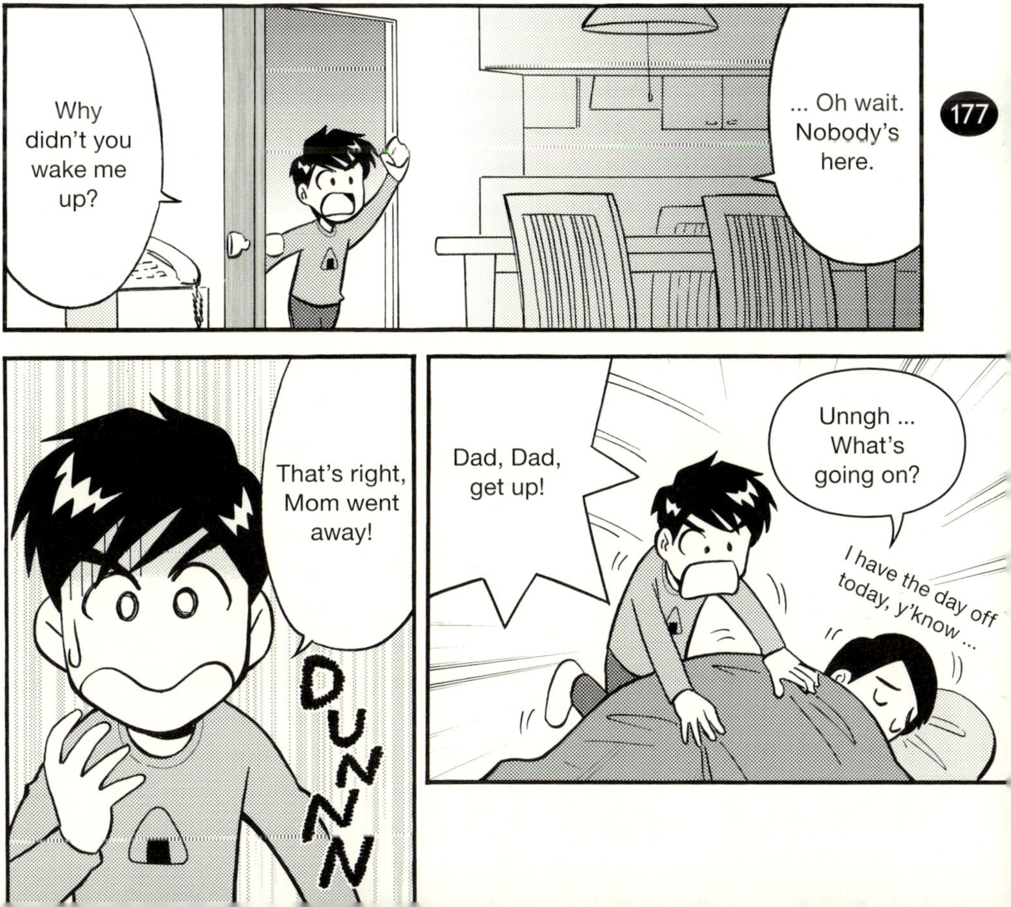

Why didn't you wake me up?

... Oh wait. Nobody's here.

That's right, Mom went away!

DUNNN

Dad, Dad, get up!

Unngh ... What's going on?

I have the day off today, y'know ...

Mom went on a trip with her friends, remember?

ding dong ♪
dang donnng

... and that's why you're late this morning?
Sorry.

And you forgot your gym clothes too?

Mom always gets them ready for me ...
Moms rock!

179

None of this would've happened if she wasn't away.
QUIVER QUIVER

It's all her fault!
grumble grumble
Wh-what?

Calm down!

180

Maybe now you see what a debt you owe your mom!

A debt?
He owes money?!

What then?
No, not money!

GRATITUDE
The Chinese character "*on*," or gratitude, consists of two elements, "cause" and "mind."

There is a cause for everything.

I guess you're right.
We feel gratitude when we come to know the cause of our blessings.
Who do you think helped you become as well off as you are now?

Think about it. Throughout our lives, we owe thanks to countless people and things!

We do?
They give us shelter and support!

Without this tree, I'd be sopping wet!
ZHHH
Trees shelter us from rain and from the burning rays of the sun in summer.

Once we all took shelter under a tree, remember?!

Without this tree, I'd have collapsed from heatstroke ...

In the same way, we are sheltered and helped in many ways in life!

Take
nature
itself.
We need sun
and water,
air, earth,
and plants
to live!

SNIIIFF
That's
for sure.

What about
the people
around you?

I'm here
thanks to
my parents,
who always
take care
of me!

I got well
thanks to
the doctor
who treated
me!

We can study
thanks to
Mr. Suzuki,
who teaches
us!
There's
no end
to it!

We tend to think that we can survive on our own ...

But our very survival depends on others' help!
It does?

Dissatisfaction comes from taking for granted the blessings of nature and other people.
What if they weren't there? Think how much you rely on them, and you can't help but be grateful!

Now that you mention it ... I always took it for granted that Mom would cook for me.

Ah, that's a sign you've changed!

Tell her thank you!
Thanks, I will!

Buddha said that "an ungrateful person is worse than a beast"! He taught us the importance of knowing gratitude, feeling gratitude, and repaying the debt of gratitude that we owe.

KNOW GRATITUDE
FEEL GRATITUDE
SHOW GRATITUDE
We need to know what to be grateful for, we need to be grateful, and we need to show our gratitude!
Yes. Buddha taught that those who feel no gratitude are lower than beasts.

184

There's a famous statue of a dog named Hachi in front of a train station in Japan.

Pretty amazing.
Faithful dog Hachi-kō
Hardly anyone— people, I mean!— gets a statue made of them!

What's this dog famous for, anyway?
SLIIIDE

Hachi went to the station every evening to meet his master.

One day his master suddenly died, and never came home again.

But for ten more years, Hachi waited every evening at the station.

Wow, he never gave up.
Such single-minded devotion is touching!
SNIFF

Yes. Even an animal knows enough to be grateful.

GRATITUDE
Great people are those who know, feel, and show gratitude!

Such people earn our trust, admiration, and respect!

What's important first and foremost is to know how much you owe others.

Mr. Suzuki, I didn't realize!

To be called an "ingrate," someone who doesn't know or feel gratitude, is a shameful thing!

No matter how much a person knows, or how wealthy he is, if he is an ingrate he is untrustworthy and pitiful!

While those who repay kindness with malice destroy themselves.

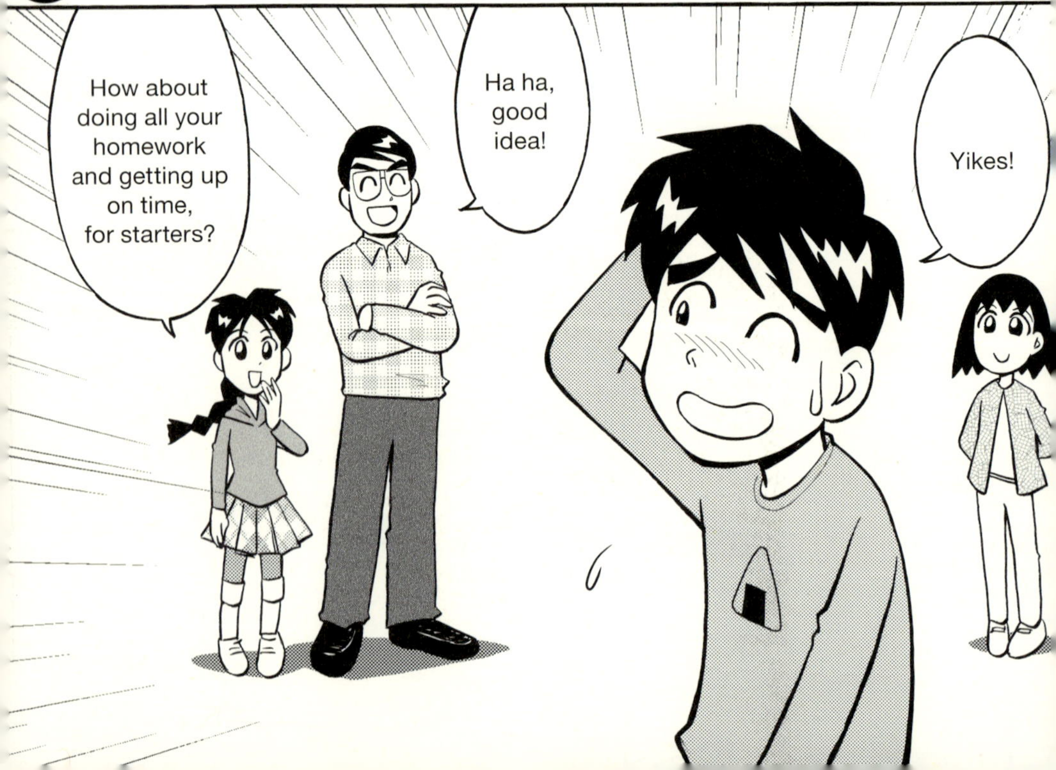

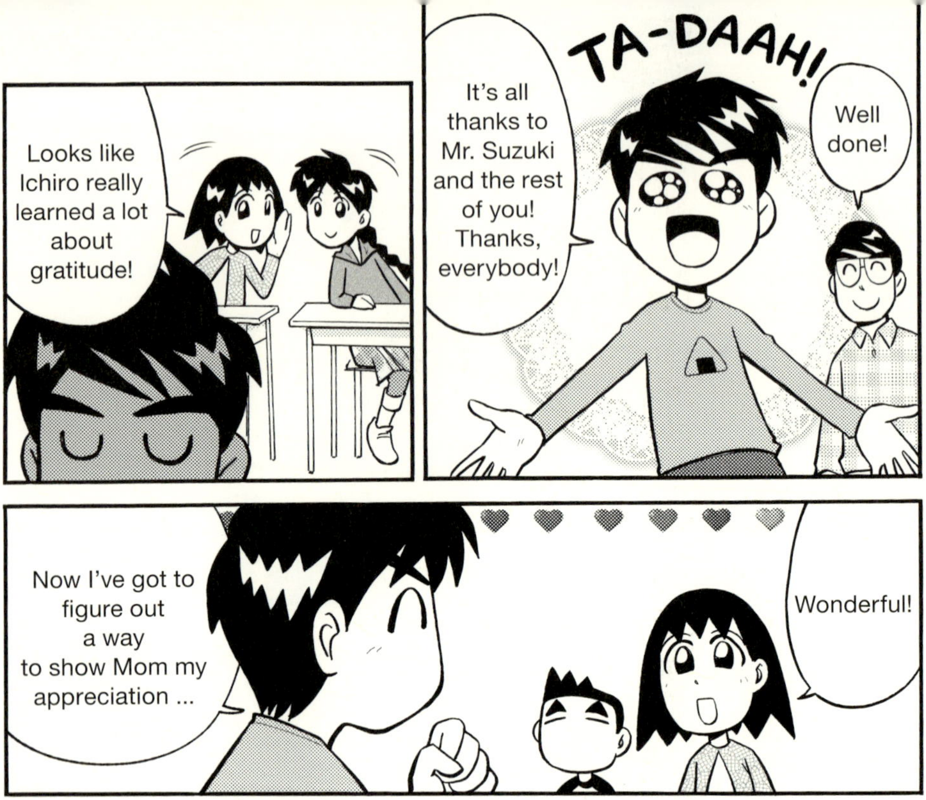

How about doing all your homework and getting up on time, for starters?

Ha ha, good idea!

Yikes!

NAGOYA STATION

I stayed up late last night studying, and overslept!

TMP TMP TMP

Yeah, right. Sure you weren't playing video games?

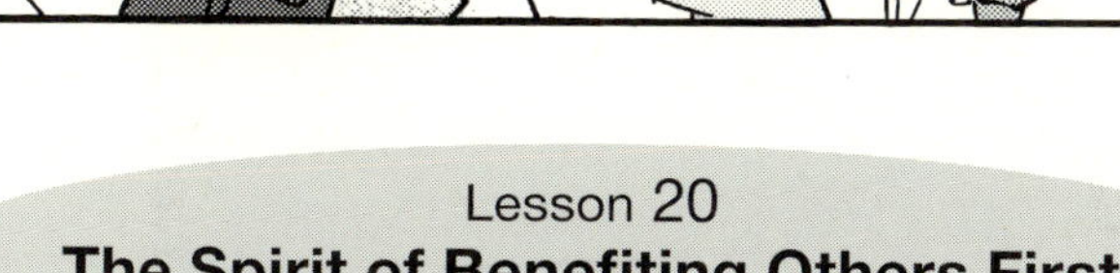

Lesson 20
The Spirit of Benefiting Others First

Being kind to others leads to your own happiness.

Ulp, how'd you know? What about you? How come you're late?

The baseball game went into extra innings ...

I couldn't go to bed without knowing who won!

CLNK

You're not so different from me!

If we don't catch the next train, we'll be late! Hurry!

Agh! Look at all these people!

MEITETSU GIFU
KANŌ
TOYO-HASHI
EX-PRESS

Hishino Nishigō
BUS S
Ichiro, you know better than to cut in line.

Yeah but ...
He doesn't get it.

You are being selfish.

?
You calling me a shellfish?
Shellfish?

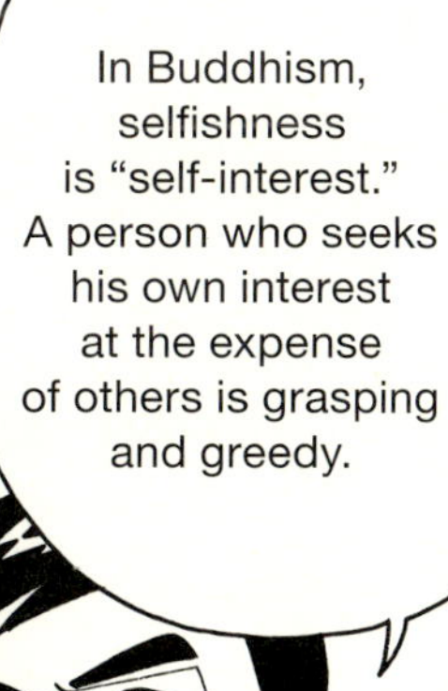

In Buddhism, selfishness is "self-interest." A person who seeks his own interest at the expense of others is grasping and greedy.

Take that back!!
BOM
Sure you don't mean Hikari? She's a crab!

Sounds like Ichiro all right!
Hey!!

Now, now. This isn't only about Ichiro, you know.

Think about it. Don't we all have this selfish mind?

Ohohoho! Not me! I am the soul of kindness, always thinking of others!
You sure?
Mmf

I gave my seat to an old lady on the train.
Oh, thank you, dear.
Here.
That was a good deed.

But you weren't pushed to the edge. Often when we are on the edge, the way Ichiro was before, we don't give others a second thought.
I'll be late!

Yes, Masako, what if you had been in my shoes? What then?
Don't put on airs!

Here's a story about what happens to selfish people.
Once a man set out to see the Land of Utmost Bliss and the Land of Suffering.

Voilà!
Laid out before them was a rich banquet.
Could this really be the Land of Suffering?

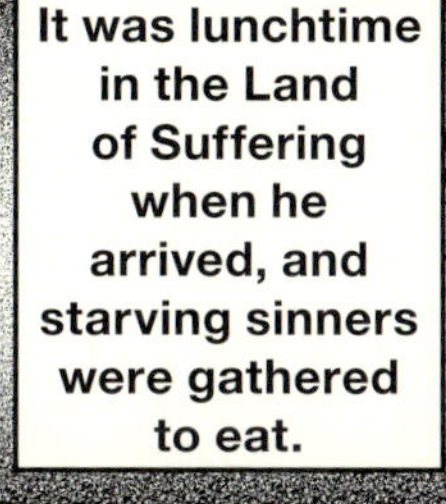
It was lunchtime in the Land of Suffering when he arrived, and starving sinners were gathered to eat.

lurch
shamble

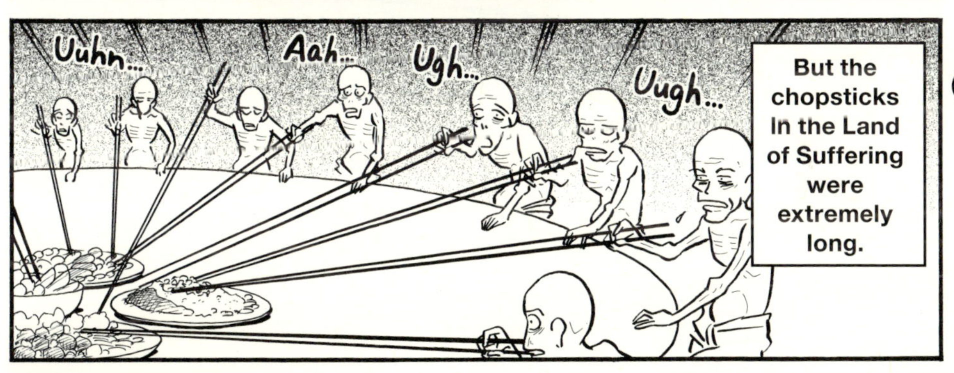
But the chopsticks in the Land of Suffering were extremely long.
Uuhn...
Aah...
Ugh...
Uugh...

193

They were so long that no one could eat with them, so the sinners only writhed in agony.
Ugh...
Agh...

When the man arrived in the Land of Utmost Bliss, it was just time for supper.

Welcome! Glad you could come!
Share our meal before you go!

The plump, well-fed residents of the Land of Utmost Bliss seated him at a rich banquet.
Here the chopsticks must be short!

NO!! They're long here too!
Hehe. Surprised?

The Land of Utmost Bliss is different from the Land of Suffering. Here we don't feed ourselves.
fwip

Of course! Here everyone uses his chopsticks to feed the one across from him!
Here you go!
Ready?
Allow me!
Thanks!

Here you go!
Yum!
CHOMP

So the difference between the Land of Utmost Bliss and the Land of Suffering is a difference in attitude.
That's what the man told himself as he went home.
When we give in to our selfishness, we create dreadful evil, and neither we nor others can be saved.
We need to do the opposite, which is benefit others and ourselves.
Others and ourselves?

Remember the story? What were the people in the Land of Utmost Bliss like?
Um ...

They fed each other with their long chopsticks.
That is benefiting others. To unselfishly make other people happy.

Benefiting others is in itself a way of benefiting ourselves.
It leads to our own happiness.
Kindness directed at others will come back to you and make you happy!
I see.

Good causes yield good results, own causes yield own results. Do something good and you reap the benefit.

It's the law of cause and effect!

Exactly right.

I won't cut in line anymore.

Let's be careful.

Let's put the spirit of benefiting others and ourselves into practice!

OK!!

HATENA

Afterword

Back when I was a child … we lived in a world without cell phones or laptop computers. We kids would gather at a neighborhood temple for "Sunday school." Such chances are few today, when temples have largely become places for funerals and memorial services. With the change in values, now even funerals are held in abbreviated style, and more and more people go through life knowing little or nothing about Buddhism. This is extremely regrettable.

Buddhism, which our ancestors cared about so much that they held Sunday school to teach it to children, has much of importance to tell us about life itself. My desire to present the teachings of Buddha in a fashion that even small children could enjoy was the starting point for these comics. Rather to my surprise, adults have responded to the content even more enthusiastically than children, calling it easy to understand and enjoyable. This brought home to me the need for readily comprehensible books that explain Buddhism.

Nothing would make me happier than for people to take this book in hand and, perhaps with a few giggles along the way, learn the crucial teachings of Buddhism—teachings that can transform lives. It is especially gratifying to think that *The ABCs of Buddhism* will be accessible through this English translation to readers not only in Japan, but around the world. Those who want to know more about Buddha himself and what sort of person he was can refer to my book *The Story of Buddha: A Graphic Biography* (Ichimannendo Publishing, Inc., 2011). To anyone who would like to dig deeper and know the purpose of life, I recommend *You Were Born for a Reason* by Kentetsu Takamori, Daiji Akehashi, and Kentaro Ito (Ichimannendo Publishing, Inc., 2006).

My earnest desire is that the Buddhist teachings of salvation for one and all may bring happiness to all people on this earth.

Hisashi Ota
March 2016

Translator's Note

Buddhism began in India more than two millennia ago and has since spread through Asia and around the world. What's it all about? This book, based on the writings of Shinran (1173–1263), the founder of True Pure Land Buddhism in Japan, sets forth the teachings of Buddha in a style that children of all ages can understand and enjoy. I hope many children and their parents will join Ichiro and his friends on this rollicking adventure through *The ABCs of Buddhism* and beyond.

I dedicate this translation with love to my grandchildren, Louise and Doris.

Juliet W. Carpenter
March 2016

About the Editorial Supervisor

Kentaro Ito

Born in Tokyo in 1969, he holds an M.A. in philosophy from the University of Tokyo. A philosopher and coauthor of *You Were Born for a Reason: The Real Purpose of Life* (Ichimannendo Publishing, Inc., 2006), he is also the author of *Otoko no tame no jibun-sagashi* [A man's journey of self-discovery], *Unmei o kirihiraku inga no hosoku* [The law of cause and effect that creates destiny], and other works.

About the Author

Hisashi Ota

Born in Shimane Prefecture in 1970, he graduated from Nagoya University's School of Science and Yoyogi Animation Academy. His other works include *The Story of Buddha: A Graphic Biography* (Ichimannendo Publishing, Inc., 2011) and *Manga rekishi jinbutsu ni manabu: Otona ni naru made ni mi ni tsuketai taisetsuna kokoro* [Learning from historical figures: Valuable lessons to take on board before adulthood—A comic] (Ichimannendo Publishing, Co. Ltd., 2016).

About the Translator

Juliet Winters Carpenter

Born in Michigan in 1948, she studied Japanese language and literature at the University of Michigan. She has translated over 60 works, including *You Were Born for a Reason*, and has won numerous awards. She is the sole person to have received the Japan-U.S. Friendship Commission Prize for the Translation of Japanese Literature twice, in 1980 and again in 2015.

Other Titles from Ichimannendo Publishing, Inc.

List Price: US$16.95
248 pages/Paperback/
8.3×5.9 inches

THE STORY OF BUDDHA

A Graphic Biography

By Hisashi Ota
Supervised by Kentaro Ito

The Buddha's life story in illustration

What are we living for? Is there meaning to life? Some twenty-five hundred years ago, in his youth Buddha had the same nagging questions that we do today.

The search for the answer to these questions is the starting point of Buddhism.

In our desire to live with strength and goodwill, the life of Buddha provides invaluable insight and guidance.

List Price: US$11.95
192 pages/Paperback/
7.4×5.1 inches

Something You Forgot ... Along the Way

Stories of Wisdom and Learning

By Kentetsu Takamori

This book introduces sixty-five heart-warming stories that show what it means to learn from life's events. These simple yet beautiful tales invite us to look deeper into almost any situation in life. In the tradition of Aesop's Fables, each story concludes with a moral lesson.

This book was originally published in Japanese by Ichimannendo Publishing Co. Ltd. It is part of a Japanese series that has sold over a million copies.

* "Ichimannen" means "ten thousand years" in Japanese and reflects the company's desire to publish books that will be cherished by readers well into the future.

Other Titles from Ichimannendo Publishing, Inc.

Why Do We Live?

YOU WERE BORN FOR A REASON

The Real Purpose of Life

By Kentetsu Takamori,
Daiji Akehashi, and Kentaro Ito

List Price: US$16.95
236 pages/Hardcover/
9.3×6.3 inches

What is the meaning of life?

Where can we find true happiness that will never fade away?

What is there in life that will never betray us, that we can devote ourselves to without regret?

These age-old questions cry out for clear answers—and this book addresses them head-on through the words of the revolutionary monk Shinran.

From the text:

"Without lasting joy or fulfillment in living, the days merge into one indistinguishable blur of eating, sleeping, and getting up. Living such a life is like running a footrace with no goal."
"French writer Albert Camus said that deep in the human heart is a 'wild longing' to know the meaning of life. We want to know, indeed we must know the meaning of life if we are to go on living."
"Once life's true purpose is known, all trouble and suffering acquires meaning. Live for life's true purpose, and all your efforts are sure to be rewarded."

★ ★ ★

YOU WERE BORN FOR A REASON is the English translation of the best-selling Japanese book on Buddhism, *Naze Ikiru,* which means "Why We Live."

You will not be the same after reading this book.

Other Titles from Ichimannendo Publishing, Inc.

List Price: US$30.00
144 pages/Hardcover/
10 x 7 inches

UNLOCKING TANNISHO
Shinran's Words on the Pure Land Path

By Kentetsu Takamori

Tannisho (Lamenting the Deviations) clarifies the heart of Pure Land Buddhism and points the way to real happiness with unforgettable expressions.
UNLOCKING TANNISHO is the only definitive commentary of this beloved classic text, and has been a remarkable success with almost a quarter of a million copies sold to date.

List Price: US$14.95
216 pages/Paperback/
7.4×5.1 inches

Unshakable Spirit
Stories of Compassion and Wisdom

By Kentetsu Takamori

Why wasn't there any rioting or looting in Japan after the devastating earthquake and tsunami of 2011?
Unshakable Spirit is a collection of heartwarming stories in which you will discover the Japanese people's underlying philosophy.

List Price: US$12.95
224 pages/Paperback/
7.4×5.1 inches

If you plant seeds of happiness, flowers of happiness will bloom

By Kazushi Okamoto

It's doing the little things today that makes your tomorrows brighter

Just as seeds cause flowers to bloom and fruit to appear, so our actions give rise to happiness or unhappiness.
If we don't sow the seeds of happiness, we will never become happy. What are the seeds of happiness?
This book guides the reader with clear and simple answers to this question.